OFFICIAL REPORT

OF THE

TWENTY - SECOND INTERNATIONAL

CHRISTIAN ENDEAVOR CONVENTION

HELD IN

THE FIFTH REGIMENT ARMORY, LYRIC HALL AND

MANY CHURCHES

BALTIMORE, MD., JULY 5-10, 1905.

First Fruits Press
Wilmore, Kentucky
c2015

First Fruits Press
The Academic Open Press of Asbury Theological Seminary
204 N. Lexington Ave., Wilmore, KY 40390
859-858-2236
first.fruits@asburyseminary.edu
asbury.to/firstfruits

Frederick Ohrenschall   J. Barry Mahool   William G. Baker   G. W. Haddaway   Spencer E. Sisco
   Henry Gilligan   W. A. Schumacher   Richard A. Harris   J. Alexander Johnson   Charles E. Ecker

Robert H. Smith   James O. Moul   W. O. Atwood   W. C. Perkins   B. A. Abbott   W. M. Robinson
   Luther E. Martin

THE BALTIMORE CONVENTION COMMITTEE

THE STORY

OF THE

BALTIMORE CONVENTION

THE OFFICIAL REPORT

OF THE

TWENTY-SECOND INTERNATIONAL

Christian Endeavor Convention

HELD IN

THE FIFTH REGIMENT ARMORY, LYRIC HALL
AND MANY CHURCHES

BALTIMORE, MD., JULY 5-10, 1905

Copyright, 1905, by the U. S. C. E.

UNITED SOCIETY OF CHRISTIAN ENDEAVOR
BOSTON, MASS.

The Plimpton Press Norwood Mass. U.S.A.

CONTENTS

	PAGE
Committee of 1905	5
Christian Endeavor Hymn by John Hay	6
In the Vestibule	7

CHAPTERS.

I.	The Opening Session	14
II.	The Praise of the Nations	26
III.	Endeavor in Meditation	31
IV.	Endeavor at Work	33
V.	For the Boys and Girls	42
VI.	A Superlative Junior Rally	47
VII.	The Brotherhood of Christian Endeavor	55
VIII.	The World-wide Brotherhood	58
IX.	Rally Day, State and Denominational	61
X.	Evangelism	71
XI.	Christian Culture for Christian Service	75
XII.	An Earned Play Day	79
XIII.	Christian Endeavor Camp-fire	82
XIV.	The Sunday Services	86
XV.	The Men's Meeting	89
XVI.	The Woman's Meeting	93
XVII.	The Boys' and Girls' Meeting	95
XVIII.	Two Great Reforms	98
XIX.	Recognition Morning	101
XX.	Christian Endeavor and Reforms	108
XXI.	The Closing Session	113
XXII.	Greetings from Many Lands	127
XXIII.	The Evangelistic Work	130
XXIV.	Convention Features	133
XXV.	The Convention Aftermath	135
Index		139

LIST OF ILLUSTRATIONS

The Baltimore Convention Committee	*Frontispiece*	
Convention Speakers	opposite page	15
Convention Speakers	"	21
In the Armory — The Chorus	"	27
A Portion of the Audience in the Armory	"	43
A View of the Ceiling Decorations	"	47
A Near View of the Chorus	"	47
Convention Speakers	"	51
An Armory Audience, from the Rear Gallery	"	57
Convention Speakers	"	61
Mt. Royal Station of the Baltimore & Ohio R.R.	"	71
Sea Lion Pond, Druid Hill Park	"	71
Mt. Vernon Place	"	79
Convention Speakers	"	89
Battle Monument and Court House	"	95
Monument to the Maryland Heroes of the Revolution	"	101
Convention Speakers	"	113
Boat Lake, Druid Hill Park	"	127
A View in Druid Hill Park	"	127

THE COMMITTEE OF 1905

EXECUTIVE OFFICERS

W. O. ATWOOD, *Chairman.*
ROBERT H. SMITH, *Vice-Chairman.*
W. M. ROBINSON, *Secretary.*
WM. G. BAKER, JR., *Treasurer.*

CHAIRMEN OF SUB-COMMITTEES

W. C. PERKINS, *Finance.*
W. A. SCHUMACHER, *Reception.*
C. E. ECKER, *Entertainment.*
FREDERICK OHRENSCHALL, *Registration.*
SPENCER E. SISCO, *Halls.*
J. BARRY MAHOOL, *Decorations.*
HENRY GILLIGAN, *Press and Publicity.*
RICHARD A. HARRIS, *Music.*
LUTHER E. MARTIN, *Printing.*
JAS. O. MOUL, *Ushers.*
J. ALEX. JOHNSON, *Excursions.*
REV. B. A. ABBOTT, *Evangelistic.*
REV. G. W. HADDAWAY, *Pulpit Supply.*

MUSICAL DIRECTORS

PERCY S. FOSTER, WASHINGTON, D. C.
F. H. JACOBS, BROOKLYN, N. Y.
RICHARD A. HARRIS, BALTIMORE, MD.

ASSISTANT DIRECTORS

W. R. HALL, BALTIMORE, MD.
ROBERT LEROY HASLUP, BALTIMORE, MD.
HARRY M. SMITH, BALTIMORE, MD.
THOS. L. THOMAS, BALTIMORE, MD.
CHAS. R. WOODS, BALTIMORE, MD.

ORGANISTS

ROBERT LEROY HASLUP, BALTIMORE, MD.
D. MERRICK SCOTT, BALTIMORE, MD.

Christian Endeavor

Hon. John Hay
(L. M.)
Percy S. Foster

1. Lord, from far-sev-ered climes we come To meet at last in Thee, our Home.
2. De-fend us, Lord, from ev-'ry ill; Strengthen our hearts to do Thy will;
3. O let us hear th'in-spir-ing word Which they of old at Ho-reb heard.
4. Thou who art Light, shine on each soul! Thou who art Truth, each mind con-trol!

Thou who hast been our guide and guard Be still our hope, our rich re-ward.
In all we plan and all we do Still keep us to Thy ser-vice true.
Breathe to our hearts the high command: "Go on-ward and pos-sess the land."
O-pen our eyes and make us see The path which leads to Heav'n and Thee.

This "Invocation Hymn" was written by Hon. John Hay for the Fifteenth International Christian Endeavor Convention at Washington, D.C., in July, 1896, but sung to an old tune. The above is the first original tune set to the hymn, and was written by Mr. Percy S. Foster, of Washington, D.C., especially for the Twenty-second International Christian Endeavor Convention at Baltimore, Md., July, 1905.

Copyright, 1905, by Percy S. Foster

IN THE VESTIBULE

Baltimore "Best Yet"

SOME ingenious and optimistic prophet in Boston predicted that the Baltimore Convention would prove to be the "best yet" in the history of Christian Endeavor, famed as that history is for great conventions. The prophecy was fully justified by the event. "Baltimore — 1905" takes its proud place in that remarkable front rank of the world's surpassing religious conventions which includes Boston, New York, Chicago, Washington, St. Louis, Detroit, San Francisco, and Denver. And Baltimore deserves the appellation conferred by William Shaw, who in the closing session pronounced it the "Superlative Convention." Let us not press too closely a broad characterization, nor let any other convention city feel a twinge of jealousy. There are adjectives enough to go around, and each convention was in its own way and year the "best yet." Let "Superlative" stand for this one, and let all rejoice in the events, numbers, spirit, and enthusiasm which made it so.

MEMORABLE AS WELL AS SUPERLATIVE

The Baltimore Convention will be memorable in Endeavor annals, first of all, because of the presentation and endorsement of the testimonial to Dr. Clark by which it is proposed to mark the completion of the first quarter century of the Christian Endeavor movement. As the report will show, this project to raise a testimonial fund for the double purpose of erecting a suitable headquarters for Christian Endeavor and securing an endowment sufficient to put the world-wide extension work of Endeavor on a permanent basis, met with most enthusiastic approval both from the Board of Trustees and the twenty thousand Endeavorers who represented the millions of members in State and Local Unions and local societies.

THE EVANGELISTIC KEYNOTE

Memorable was the Convention also for its evangelistic keynote. This was struck in President Clark's address, one of the most stirring calls he has ever made for church advancement, and was heard all through the Convention, finding its culmination in that wonderful Men's Meeting in the Armory on Sunday afternoon, when a revival wave such as was never witnessed in a young people's gathering swept over the thousands of men, moving hundreds of them towards the haven of salvation.

New Plan of Registration

Memorable, again, this Convention, because here for the first time the plan of partial self-support was put into practice in regard to Convention expenses. The dollar fee for registration, in return for which the delegates received badge, official souvenir program, guide-book to the city, map, and a copy of the official report, was a novel feature. This is the English fashion, and Baltimore experience assures its success. Endeavorers will be more self-respecting for bearing a fair share of the necessarily heavy expenses attendant upon such vast meetings. The great majority of them registered, and when the plan was made known to them heartily endorsed it.

The Musical Convention

Superlative surely in its musical features was this Convention. The great chorus of twenty-four hundred voices, not counting a thousand Juniors, was thoroughly drilled and had a volume unsurpassed for richness and harmonious blending of tones. Then the high character of the music! It was a constant inspiration to see and hear that vast choir, and all those who have sought to raise the standard of music in our societies have reason to be grateful to the musical leaders of Baltimore. Mr. Harris led the regular choir and Mr. Porter the Juniors, and their selections illustrated the inspiring and satisfying and also interesting quality of anthems and hymns of the first order of good music. The congregational hymns, too, from the Endeavor Hymnal, were as effective as leaders like Mr. Foster and Mr. Jacobs know how to make them; while Mr. Jacobs was in the "superlative" mood and voice in his solos, which were repeatedly encored. Taken altogether, it is doubtful whether sacred music has ever been made more impressive. Baltimore will go down as the great Musical Convention.

Superlative in Audiences

Christian Endeavor is accustomed to immense gatherings, and looks back to fifty-eight thousand at Boston as a record maker. But those thousands never saw a single mass meeting like this at Baltimore. The audiences at former conventions had to be divided up into two or three tents and a series of halls and churches. In Baltimore the massive Fifth Regiment Armory was fitted up to seat sixteen thousand people, and it was full to standing room on several occasions, so that one had the inspiring sight of some eighteen thousand persons under the one roof. What if it was often impossible to hear the speakers, it was possible to see, and the sight of such a Christian host was enough to make one grow large with faith and hope and cheer as the significance of it was realized. And when that mighty company sang, as they did sing, that was congregational singing indeed! Such vast congregations make irresistibly for enthusiasm; and when patriotism was aroused, as during the festival of song, the effect was thrilling. So Baltimore will stand first for immense numbers in a single audience.

A "Spell" of Weather

It was simply marvelous how these audiences kept up in face of a record-breaking week of weather. Christian Endeavor has been ac- accustomed to some hot days and occasionally some wet days during Convention week, but never to such a week as this. The remark was repeatedly made that no other convention but one of Christian Endeavor young people would have sustained such discomfort and maintained attendance and enthusiasm. Rain, rain, rain, downpours amounting to floods; humidity up in the nineties and the thermometer mercury ranging up in the same high and sweltering altitudes; thunder storms without warning; alternate baking and wetting — it did seem as though Baltimore was compressing all the bad weather of a year into a few days. But Endeavorers were everywhere, and so were smiling faces, and the severe test of strength and patience was borne in such wise as to call forth common commendation among the citizens. As Dr. Smith Baker, of the Williston Society, said: "What has astonished me most is the way the people have come out to meetings in spite of the rain. That element would have dampened the ardor of any other convention, and might possibly have made the whole thing a failure, but in this case it hardly kept anybody from the events." And the portly Portland pastor, described by the Baltimore reporters as "resembling Henry Ward Beecher," was among those whom neither heat nor wet could keep at home. He said a preacher who didn't perspire couldn't inspire and ought to expire.

A Wonderful Spectacle

The scenic effects at the Armory were wonderful. The arrangement of the seats made the great hall look like the oblong of a football field; with the surrounding tiers of seats rising to lofty height. Back of the platform at one end were the choir seats, with the splendid organ, built especially for the occasion by a Maryland firm, in the center. The side and rear galleries completed the amphitheater, so that the speakers stood in an enclosing circle of humanity, with a plain of people in front of them. Thrilling it was to look out upon that intense, eager, responsive throng, made up distinctively of young people, and largely of young men. It was worth using up one's voice in the effort to make them hear.

The Decorator's Skill

Superlative in taste and lavishness were the decorations. Red, white, and blue streamers swung down from the lofty arches of the roof. Everywhere the red and white of Christian Endeavor was set off strikingly by the yellow and black of Maryland, producing the most artistic and harmonious color effects. The flags of many nations were to be seen, illustrating the international phase of Endeavor. Electricity was employed in superlative degree. On the Armory roof were the letters "C. E." in gigantic size, while at the State headquarters and from a number of public buildings the same letters shone forth at night in brilliancy. Elaborate electrical designs on the wall in the rear of the platform never failed to draw rounds of applause at the opening of the evening sessions. The decorations around the galleries were especially effective. At intervals the stars and stripes were combined with the union jack, and between, in great letters, were the words, "Worship God." That was the only motto. The idea was reverential, and reverence resulted, as the eye rested again and again upon the words. How much the motto had to do with it one cannot say, but never has there been a more seriously purposeful and reverent convention. One of the superlatives might properly be put to that; and it gave a cumulative blessed influence to the sessions, until the Convention pinnacle was reached. It was a week's dwelling in a higher world.

Lyric Hall

This gem of a meeting place, a little way from the Armory, was exquisite in its decorations. "Gem" may not be exactly the word for a hall seating three thousand people, but it seemed small and delightfully cozy and homelike after the vast Armory. Crowded it was on the evenings when it served for the simultaneous meetings; and the two halls crowded gave combined numbers considerably exceeding twenty thousand at these evening sessions. That, too, when the excessive and exhaustive heat and humidity made breathing not the easiest of exercises, because there seemed little to breathe.

Great in Numbers

It may as well be said here that those who coddle the notion that great mass meetings of Christian Endeavorers are things written in the past tense should kindly take notice. The most conservative estimate — not guesswork, but based on registration, railroad tickets presented, and careful counts — shows that the total attendance was about twenty thousand. This made it a hard convention for the croaker and the pessimist in general. If he was in Baltimore, the superlative conditions led him to careful concealment. The atmosphere may have been sticky and uncomfortable, but it was too heavily charged with cheer and joy, enthusiasm and evangelism, for misanthropy. Numbers come, and numbers count, and never was there a more convincing proof of the inherent vitality and vigor of the Christian Endeavor movement than was given at Baltimore. The biennial convention, moreover, approves itself; as appetite grows during the off year. Nor must it be forgotten that a new generation is rising, fresh for convention experiences.

Superlative Hospitality

Baltimore is a hospitable city. Its hospitality has the graciousness and courtesy and polish of the South in it. It envelops the visitor like an atmosphere. The incomers were met by the Reception Committees, and attended in person to their various State Headquarters. There were hundreds of workers on the Reception Committee, as there were hundreds of white-capped ushers, who were wholly devoted to their duties, and as pleasant as they were untiring. It is said that one delegation was announced to arrive at a certain hour twelve hundred strong, and the committee at the church made all preparations for such a host, and then waited. The hour came, the delegation did not come; the hosts did not dare go away from headquarters, lest their guests arrive, and find no greeting; so the loyal Baltimoreans went without dinner and waited until late at night, hours after the appointed time, At last a straggling fifty arrived. Trains belated, plans frustrated. but not a groan. That was the spirit of a splendid service by hundreds who did not have any chance to enjoy the sessions at the Armory because of their duties as hosts at headquarters. That is Baltimorean hospitality. The brand is warranted pure, and ought to be imported into every part of the land. There was no lack of homes in which to place visitors; no lack of anything in the way of kindness and politeness and attentiveness.

Provincial Pride

Baltimoreans are proud of their city. They take a provincial pride in it, and provincial pride makes a place desirable to live in. Kindly provincialism is preferable to selfish cosmopolitanism every time. There is abundant reason for the pride. There are fine monuments well placed in little squares; educational institutions, hospitals, and philanthropic organizations abound; church spires and towers are to be seen in all sections, generally conspicuous. A city of homes, schools, and churches — why not a city to like? The new business Baltimore, rising on the ashes of the burnt Baltimore, will show blocks of fine architecture, a vast improvement on the old.

Freedom of the City

Mayor and Governor extended the freedom of the city and the commonwealth, and the people seconded them. A large number of the business houses decorated their buildings in honor of the visitors, and the red and white, with the familiar monogram, were in evidence also at the railway stations and on the public buildings. The city authorities, indeed, appropriated $1,500 for decorations, and the city hall had an elaborate design on its façade, while its dome was dazzlingly lighted by 3,000 electric bulbs at night, so that the city's official welcome was prominent at all hours. The wearing of a badge was sufficient to command attention from not only police, motormen, and other public servants, but from the citizens, who answered the most foolish questions with model courtesy. All this made the stay in the city exceedingly pleasant.

Graceful and Generous

Superlative was the hospitality of the Fifth Regiment. The fact should be widely known and appreciated that this military organization freely gave up its Armory to the Convention. Not only was the great hall surrendered to the peaceful army of invading Endeavorers, but the companies turned themselves out of their company rooms, affording ample facilities for registration and committee rooms, the Endeavor exhibit and missionary museum, press and trustee rooms, writing rooms, and down-stairs a great dining hall. Hearty thanks to the gallant Fifth from the millions of Endeavorers!

The City Press

The morning papers, the *American* and *Sun*, not only gave pages of space to the Convention, but editorially and reportorially maintained a sympathetic attitude that was especially gratifying. Such reports and editorials could not fail to deepen the influence of the Convention upon the people of the city. It was an intelligent appreciation of the true character and weight of the Christian Endeavor movement. And if the reporters insisted upon erecting a two million dollar building as a tribute to Dr. Clark, that only proves how generous they felt towards the society and its leaders, and how large Endeavor looms to them. The evening papers, the *Herald* and *News*, were equally friendly and sympathetic. Great credit is due to the genial chairman of the publicity committee, Mr. Gilligan, for the interest taken by the papers in the Convention. The Baltimore press, including the Associated Press representative, deserves all praise for its attitude towards moral and religious questions, and for its general high moral tone. Evidently the people will not support yellow journalism, greatly to their credit. Newspapers advertise a city in more ways than one. Here are examples of editorial utterance worthy of preservation: —

Dauntless and Thorough

The Christian Endeavorers have proved themselves to be thoroughly in their work in their late Convention. Since they have assembled here they have been tried by heat and flood and neither the one nor the other has succeeded in drying up their energy or drowning out their enthusiasm in the good cause to which they have devoted themselves. The city ought to be the better for their visit and the example they have given of single-hearted devotion to their aims and the unselfish disregard of their own comfort under rather trying conditions.

Honored Guests

Baltimore extends a cordial welcome to each and all of the Christian Endeavorers. It greets them as guests it delights to honor, and sincerely hopes that nothing will occur to mar the pleasure, enjoyment, or profit of any individual. As the aims and work of this organization have become better known the people have gained a true appreciation of its real value as a religious agency and as a powerful factor in the uplifting and betterment of the human race. It binds itself to no creed, limits itself to no sect, but invites all who hold to the fundamental principles and teachings of the Christian religion to join with it in the work it is doing so well. Such a body of earnest men and women must ever be welcome in any American city, and Baltimore means this week to show that it is not unmindful of the honor of being chosen as the Convention city of 1905.

"Wide Open"

Baltimore greets the incoming hosts of Christian Endeavorers. During their stay it will be wide open in the best sense of the word. It can feel that the young people thronging its streets will be alert for the things which interest and elevate. If Baltimore cannot demonstrate to them ample reasons for the conclusion that it is one of the most hospitable, in its residential and suburban sections beautiful, and in its location, contiguous to the Chesapeake Bay, attractive cities in the country, it has greatly overestimated its points of appeal.

It is impossible that they should get close enough into the spirit of Baltimore to catch the newer Baltimore hustle which is making the dust fly in the burnt district in evidence of its determination to have a bigger and better city which shall merit the prophetic eulogy of its beloved poet Sidney Lanier:

"The world has bloomed again at Baltimore."

Preliminary Meetings

On the Friday evening preceding the Convention the chorus gave a concert which was attended by fully fifteen thousand people. That was one evidence of Baltimore's interest. The proof of the performance lies in the fact that the people urged a repetition of the concert after the Convention, and this was arranged for, at popular prices.

On Sunday evening before the Convention, moreover, there was a fellowship meeting, at which the auditorium was crowded to listen to brief addresses on Christian unity from leading pastors of various denominations, representing the United Evangelistic Campaign Committee, which has planned a two months' series of services in a half dozen different parts of the city. All hoped the Endeavor Convention would start the revival movement gloriously, and so it did, as the Men's Meeting showed.

Now to the Convention. Let us pass from the vestibule within the temple of praise and worship.

CHAPTER I

The Opening Session

THE ARMORY, WEDNESDAY AFTERNOON

THINGS were doing Wednesday morning. Delegates were hurrying into Baltimore by the trainload. Reception committees were busy at the stations and at the nineteen churches where State headquarters had been established. Those who came on Tuesday were seeing the city, and those arriving were seeing where they were to be located. The United Society was holding its annual meeting, and the Trustees later were most heartily making their own in official wise the suggestion that the twenty-fifth year of Christian Endeavor be worthily signalized by a testimonial to its beloved founder and leader which should give permanence to the great movement. At the Armory the last touches were being made in preparation for the start.

It was humid and torrid and horrid convention weather. While the Endeavorers were gathering the clouds were gathering also, and at the time when the thousands were setting out for the Armory the bottom of the sky seemed to fall out and the rain came in torrents. But the undaunted Endeavorers came, too, just as though the sun shone, and as the rain poured down they poured in, until it was evident that the meeting was going to be a great one for the first day. Many trains and delegations were known to be belated, yet at three o'clock thousands were in place to hear the resounding tones of the massive organ, and to join in the praise service which that stanch musical Endeavorer, Mr. Percy S. Foster, led. From the very beginning the old-time convention enthusiasm was manifest. Endeavor leaders of experience in conventions knew what it meant when the company began to sing with a will and a heart in it; but it will be good to show here how the scene impressed the *Sun* reporter, new to such experiences. This is his graphic description:—

> In the presence of 10,000 people from every State in the Union and from every land and clime the Twenty-second International Convention was formally opened. While the rain fell in torrents the thunderous tones of the organ swelled

Rev. Carey Bonner

Prof. H. B. Grose

THE ARMORY

Rev. C. H. Tyndall

Richard A. Harris

through and through the vast auditorium, and the voices of thousands were lifted up in glad praise. Dripping, but undismayed; dauntless in their courage and enthusiasm; undiscouraged by the heat, unterrified by the storm, the Christian hosts flocked to the opening session with hearts attuned to the melody of the moment and souls alive to the greatness of their cause. The huge hall, beautiful and gay with its graceful drapery of many hues; its fluttering flags and waving banners, its gleaming emblems of city, state, and nation; its inspiring, all-embracing motto: "The World for Christ," in bright, white letters high above the throng, was a fitting frame for the great gathering within.

Men and women and children of all nations sat on the stage and in the big body of the hall. Young and old, grave and gay, the strong and the weak, mingled together, sitting on the rough chairs, singing shoulder to shoulder, cheering with the vim of soldiers on the firing line and simultaneously bowing their heads in silent prayer. Permeating the whole assembly was that wonderful Christian Endeavor spirit which has caused the influence of that small band of earnest young men and women, who twenty-four years ago formed the nucleus of the present organization, to spread the whole world round, until there is not now a civilized country where the work and the meaning of the Society are not known. When the Convention was called to order the scene within the armory was an inspiring one and could not fail to thrill those who gazed upon it and realized the meaning and significance of the gathering.

That is true enough. The sight of the chorus clad in white was enough to make one forget the heat, and the sound of the chorus made the pulses beat quick. As the platform filled applause kept breaking out as newcomers were recognized. The Mayor blushed becomingly at his reception, while the Governor, coming at the psychological moment, was inspired by the warm greeting for his welcome address — welcome in every sense.

The mighty volume of sound of the opening hymn, the Doxology, drowned the noise of the rain, which fell like a shower of bullets on the roof, making the voice in speech almost inaudible. The chair was taken by Rev. Howard B. Grose, of New York, vice-president of the Board of Trustees and one of the Old Guard of original Trustees, whose skill in presiding has often been proved, and then the first and only shadow fell upon the Convention as the people learned that Dr. Clark would not be present. But in obedience to what everybody knew would be his most earnest desire, not even this was permitted to affect the Convention spirit injuriously. The invocation was offered by Dr. Floyd W. Tomkins, of Philadelphia, who led the audience in the Lord's Prayer in closing.

"In the absence of our loved leader, through illness, an absence as profoundly regretted by us all as by himself," said the presiding officer, "it is my pleasant duty to declare the Twenty-second International Convention of Christian Endeavor now open."

The following message was read from Dr. Clark, and was received with deep sympathy:

PINE POINT, ME., July 5, 1905.

My dear Friends, —

I am facing this afternoon one of the keenest sorrows and disappointments of my life, in deciding that I cannot go to Baltimore for the Convention to which I have been looking forward, and for which I have been preparing for many months past. But my health does not allow it, and friends and physicians all unite in forbidding me to go. My prayer shall be for the Convention hour by hour, and I ask a remembrance in your prayers, that I may soon be able again to take up my share of the work for Christian Endeavor which God has committed to us all.

With sincere regard and affection for all,

Faithfully yours,
FRANCIS E. CLARK.

Immediately upon the reading of this message, President George B. Stewart, of Auburn Theological Seminary, offered a feeling prayer for Dr. Clark. "Lord, he whom Thou lovest is sick," he urged, and pleaded for a speedy restoration to health.

Now came the opportunity, singularly made by circumstances, to pay tribute to that Christian statesman, John Hay. Nothing could have been more felicitous and fitting. The devotional exercises were to have been conducted by Dr. Teunis S. Hamlin, who was at that hour conducting a memorial service for his parishioner and friend, the late Secretary of State. Another Washington minister, who was President Garfield's pastor, Dr. F. D. Power, was present, and took Dr. Hamlin's place. He led the great congregation in the recitation of the first psalm, so appropriate to the lamented statesman, and followed with prayer. Professor Grose voiced the common sorrow at the loss of such a man, whose passing made the world appreciably poorer, and announced that the Christian Endeavor hymn which Secretary Hay wrote for the Washington Convention in 1896 had been set to music by Mr. Foster especially for this Convention, and would now be sung. He called attention to the fourth verse, as already realized by the writer:—

> Thou who art Light, shine on each soul!
> Thou who art Truth, each mind control!
> Open our eyes and make us see
> The path which leads to Heaven and Thee.

The great audience rose and, led by Mr. Foster, who wrote the tune, sang touchingly the beautiful hymn, beginning,

> Lord, from far severed climes we come
> To meet at last in Thee, our Home.
> Thou who hast been our guide and guard
> Be still our hope, our rich reward.

"We have come to the time of salutations," said the chairman, "and as Christian Endeavor is international it is fitting that the first welcome should be national, at least, from an international favorite. We will first hear from President Roosevelt"—and as necks were craned in surprise he added, "through his representative, William Shaw." When the laughter ceased, amid silence that made the after applause seem all the louder, this message was read:—

OYSTER BAY, N. Y., July 4, 1905.
REV. FRANCIS E. CLARK, D. D.,
President United Society of Christian Endeavor, Baltimore, Md.

I am very sorry that it has been found impossible for me to accept your invitation to address the Christian Endeavor Convention. But will you permit me to send through you a word of greeting to those assembled, and to heartily wish them continued success in the work in which they are engaged? The work of your Society during the quarter of a century of its existence has been far-reaching in its effect for good. To make better citizens, to lift up the standard of American manhood and womanhood, is to do the greatest service to the country. The stability of this government depends upon the individual character of its citizenship. No more important work can be done, important to the cause of Christianity as well as to our national life and greatness.

THEODORE ROOSEVELT.

The Endeavorers rose and cheered and waved their handkerchiefs in honor of the absent "first American of the century." Mr. Shaw proposed that he be authorized to send the following reply, and the Convention responded with a will that left no doubt as to its sentiments:—

BALTIMORE, MD., July 5, 1905.
PRESIDENT THEODORE ROOSEVELT,
President's Train, Lake Shore Railway, Cleveland, O.

Thousands of Christian Endeavorers from many lands honor with you the memory of Secretary Hay.

We thank you for your inspiring message.

We beg you to stop at Baltimore on your way home and let us hear your voice in a plea for the nobler citizenship you exemplify.

Any hour, day or night, will do.

WILLIAM SHAW.

The enthusiasm had by this time risen to a height that defied the noise of the rain on the roof, and the way was well paved for Maryland's chief executive, a typically handsome and courteous Southern gentleman, who captivated all, and certainly ought to have been flattered at the greeting given him by that splendid chorus, which represented the famed beauty of Baltimore femininity.

"It is good sometimes to make random inquiries," said the chairman, introducing the Governor. "Christian Endeavor is not a political or a sectarian organization, but one of its fundamental principles is Christian citizenship. Meeting a citizen, a stranger, I asked him what kind of a man the Governor was. 'One of the best and most popular governors Maryland ever had,' was the prompt reply." This sentiment was vociferously applauded, and as the Governor came forward the entire throng rose and gave the Chautauqua salute, with cheers. He looked in front at the waving white, then back at the choir, and showed that he felt deeply the ovation. When he found chance, in his ringing voice he began, but applause checked him at the end of his first sentence, and his speech was punctuated in this manner all the way through. Here is the welcome entire:—

Many notable conventions, political, fraternal and religious, have met in our beautiful Baltimore, but not one so large or so international in its character as this. Every continent, every empire, every republic, every isle of the sea, every State and Territory of our Union, is represented here. Lo! an avalanche of Christianity is upon us.

I am delighted to greet such splendid soldiers of the Cross, and on behalf of every creed and faith, every race and nationality of our people, I welcome you to Maryland and extend to you the hospitality of our homes. Nothing delights Marylanders more than to have visitors, strangers, with us, especially Christian Endeavorers, because we enjoy your good fellowship, profit by your moral influence, and admire the enthusiastic way you are working for the uplifting of humanity.

I have never before stood face to face with such an immense body of earnest Christian workers. You have the red blood of youth in your veins, and the spirit of high resolve and noble self-sacrificing purpose in your hearts. You are winning success for your cause, and peace and happiness follow in the wake of your victories, — that "peace which passeth all understanding."

The growth of your Society during its twenty-four years of life has been marvelous. Born on the coast of Maine, it has reached out to the uttermost bounds of the globe, bringing into its fold and converting to its faith the natives of every clime. From the little band of fifty boys and girls who met in Williston Church, Portland, Maine, on February 2, 1881, you have, under the able leadership of your founder, Dr. Francis E. Clark, grown to a membership of over four millions. You have broken down denominational barriers and brought into harmony and united action leading Christian forces throughout the world. You have, by your self-sacrificing earnestness, aroused the dormant spirit and fervor of the older members of many Christian communities.

You have demonstrated the force of youthful enthusiasm in church work. You have become the mainstay, the hope, the sheet-anchor, as it were, of Christianity. With such a record and such a position in the church, the power you exert for the welfare of every people is great.

Therefore, you can understand why I am here, as Governor of Maryland, to welcome you to our State and thank you for the splendid influence of your presence with us. I regret that Dr. Clark is not here to-day. I wanted to meet him, shake him by the hand, and thank him for what he has done for our nation. He has won, and deserves, the gratitude of every Christian and good citizen. No American has done better service for his country. He will go down into history as one of our great benefactors.

I came here, not to recount the story of your organization, but simply to tell you how glad we are to have you with us. Maryland is an old historic State, one of the original Thirteen. She has a proud record, and has always been noted for her conservative tendencies and liberal laws.

I wish to impress upon you the fact, which should be of special interest to you Christian workers, that the government of Maryland was laid deep in the foundation of liberty of conscience and religious freedom, giving to every man the right to worship God in accordance with the dictates of his own conscience; that Maryland was the cradle of Presbyterianism in America, the first regularly constituted church of that denomination in this country having been erected at Rehoboth, on the eastern shore; that the Methodist Episcopal Church of America was established in Maryland, and its first house of worship was built upon her soil; that the first bishop of the Episcopal Church, consecrated in America, was a native Marylander and resided in this State; that the first archbishop of the Roman Catholic Church in the United States was a Marylander, and the first American cardinal is a native of our State and has his official residence here. I mention these facts because they are a part of the history of Christianity in America. It is most appropriate that in such a State, with such a religious history, your great Convention should be held.

Before I conclude I wish to refer to Mr. Atwood and his associates, who have had charge of the arrangements for this Convention. Their work has been well done. They are the kind of men we have in Maryland, splendid examples of Maryland ability and energy, and true types of the Maryland gentleman.

Believe me when I say that we are all enjoying and profiting by the religious services that your coming has inspired in this city, and I hope that you will return to us in the near future. You have won our hearts and the doors of our homes will be wide open to receive you. Wishing you godspeed in your great work, I now leave you in the hands of our genial Mayor. I commend to you as a motto for the Convention the three big "C's" — "Christ, and our Church, and our Country."

It was all so hearty and genuine, so different from the perfunctory official welcome, that again the applause rang out. During the address the Governor had kept turning toward the choir, which led the chairman to remark, "It is not strange the Governor should have been unable to keep his eyes to the front, since he had the belles of Baltimore at his back." This brought the choir to quick response, and the audience sent it back ringingly. Then, as though spontaneously, to the always inspiring tune of "Maryland" the chorus sang its welcome, adapted by Miss Amanda Harker,

> File into rank for Christ to-day,
> O Maryland, dear Maryland;
> Free to the breeze His banners play,
> Maryland, dear Maryland.
> Your noblest work for Him be done
> From early dawn to setting sun,
> Nor cease till latest victory's won,
> Maryland, my Maryland.

Mayor Timanus was introduced as the genial mayor to whom Baltimore owed its unwonted quiet on the Fourth, since he had forbidden the use of explosives. He was warmly received, and after explaining his Fourth of July order and the enforcement of it by the police who were under the Governor's control, he said the Endeavorers had the freedom of the city, and could make all the noise they wanted to without any danger of arrest. He hoped they would sing in the streets, and make the welkin ring. He spoke of the great fire and the remarkable rapidity with which the new city was arising. He said the city's appropriation of $1,500 for decorations in honor of the Convention was made with his hearty approval, and he was sure the city would reap great advantage by the presence of such a host. "I am glad to see so many Christian Endeavorers here to-day," said he, "as it would be impossible for one to meet this great concourse without being thereby made better."

The ministers and churches of Baltimore were next represented by Rev. Oliver Huckel, whose reception was not less cordial than that given to the officials. Here are two paragraphs:

We welcome you in the name of all our churches of all denominations. We welcome you without thought of denominations at all, for we are all one in Jesus Christ. We welcome you not as strangers, but as friends — not merely as friends, but as brothers and sisters in the one loving family of the Lord. We welcome you for the cause that you represent, the absolute consecration and valiant service for Christ of all the young people of the churches. We welcome you for the lofty faith, the splendid courage, and the whole-souled enthusiasm that you bring. You are in yourselves a glowing prophecy of the future, your hearts beat high with the coming victories of the church. You are the leaders of the future, the best workers in the churches, the pick of the century, the flower of the youth and chivalry of our age. We welcome you as witnesses to the perpetual youth and undying power of the Gospel of Christ.

I bid the critics who croak about the decay of Christianity to come and look into your glowing faces. You bring visions of things to come. You are already having a fulfilment among you of the ancient prophecy, "Your young men shall see visions, and on my handmaidens I will pour out in those days of my Spirit." We welcome you to all that the churches of this city can possibly do for your comfort, your entertainment, your inspiration! We are yours in heart and soul, as we belong, and rejoice to belong, to our Lord Jesus Christ.

There was one more welcome, and that from the whole-souled chairman of the Baltimore Committee, Mr. W. O. Atwood. That he is a favorite in his own city was at once evident by the quick rise of the choir and the oubturst from all over the house. He spoke from the heart. Here is a sample:

It is my happy part to express the welcome felt in the hearts of the "Committee of 1905," and the hundreds of workers who have assisted in preparing for this Convention, a happy and yet almost impossible task. For twenty months we have been preparing for this Convention, corresponding, planning, organizing, meeting, working some by day and much by night, overcoming, traveling — all for the arrival of this day. The great fire stepped in our path and plunged us into dismay; not baffled, we gathered ourselves together, and, with new plans under new conditions, pressed on; twenty months of many discouragements, yet all overcome, by God's grace; twenty months of hard work, yet with strength to acaccomplish it, with God's grace; twenty months of joy and anticipation, now realized by God's grace.

The word of welcome is difficult only because of the fulness of our hearts. We feel more like standing in silence before this vast gathering, our hearts being too full for speech. When we realize in the coming of this Convention the higher exultation of Christ, and when we hear in the tramp of your thousands the stately footsteps of Jesus; when we think of the spiritual power that must be generated here and the consecration of earnest souls to a greater service for the Master, then it is that our very being seems to burst, as it would give vent to its shout of welcome. Then, Endeavorers, from our land and from over the world, we welcome you, because of your throng; we welcome you, because of your inspiring and eloquent speakers, but THRICE WELCOME because your coming brings us in closer touch with God.

Now it was time for the response to all this hospitable greeting. President Clark was to have made it. "Since Dr. Clark is obliged to forego this pleasant task," said the chairman, "if the whole land were searched for a substitute, none other could so fittingly be chosen as the man I have the pleasure to introduce — the pastor of the original Williston Endeavor Society in Portland, Maine — Dr. Smith Baker." This is the way he impressed the *American* reporter:

Dr. Smith Baker, pastor of the mother church of the Society, who responded on the part of the visitors, was the most striking figure of all those who yesterday spoke in the Convention, possessing, in addition to a most picturesque and vener-

Hon. Charles J. Bonaparte

Hon. Henry B. F. Macfarland

Governor Warfield

Percy S. Foster

Mayor Timanus

able bearing, a keen wit and broad mental grasp. Coming from the old church of Williston, Maine, where the Christian Endeavor Society was given birth, the very personality of the quaint New England town seemed to cling to him, and his delicately-turned humorous comparisons between New England and Southern institutions and customs made him an acquaintance of the Convention as soon as he began to speak.

"We expected just such a welcome," said Mr. Baker, "and we would have been disappointed if we had met with any less wonderful hospitality in the State of Maryland. I thought before I came that it was something to be a Puritan, and that New England had some historic traditions of value, but after hearing your Governor speak upon Maryland, I have to make my bow to you. It is somewhat appropriate that I should be here to-day to tell of Williston; to tell you that the Williston Endeavor Society is as earnest to-day as it was twenty-five years ago; to tell you that the Williston Society in its lifework has answered all objections ever brought against the Society at large."

"I say to his Excellency and to his Honor that to-day they have spoken to the representatives of good citizenship, good politicians, good merchants, good lawyers, and good neighbors. They did not speak to the past, nor even to the present, but to the future, for we are the future. We want you to understand that the Christian Endeavorers here represent 7,000,000 young people all over the world. You have been talking to the future politicians and citizens of not only this country, but the whole world. We thank you for your hearty welcome, and will try to make enough noise while here, your Honor, to show you that we are having a good time."

Dr. Baker brought the house down by telling the story of the small boy who was on a Thanksgiving Day visit to his grandmother's. Seeing the loaded table, he sighed as he said, "Granny, I wish I was twins!" In view of the great feast before us, Dr. Baker said each delegate present wished he was twins.

When the applause subsided, the chorus for the first time revealed its power to render sacred music. Gounod's anthem, "Send out thy light," was sung in an unforgetable manner. It was a song sermon, and the audience could hear, which was more than a good many had been able to do, since the rain patter continued.

Secretary Vogt received a greeting which proved the place he has made for himself in the affection of Endeavorers by his manliness and modest assertiveness and broad grasp of the situation. He put vim into his report, especially in the closing part, which was a thoughtful outlook. Here is his Annual Review of the Field:

In the spirit of thanksgiving I submit to you two statements, a summary of the statistical situation, and a brief statement of impressions received by personal inquiry and touch with the work of Christian Endeavor.

I. — STATISTICAL RECORD

There are to-day 66,772 societies of Christian Endeavor: 49,339 are in the United States and Canada, and 17,433 in other lands. The ten denominations in the United States which have the largest numbers in the order named are Presbyterian, Congregational, Disciples of Christ, Baptist, Cumberland Presbyterian, Methodist Protestant, Lutheran, Dutch Reformed, Methodist Episcopal, and United Brethren. In Canada the Methodists lead, followed by the Presbyterians. The Young People's societies number 46,859, Junior 17,838, and Intermediate 1,956.

Increase at Home

After removing from the lists all societies in neglected districts that for any cause we know to have been disbanded or withdrawn from our interdenominational fellowship, the net gain for the year has been 2,014.

Increase in the States

At Denver, after a few months of the Increase Campaign, eighteen States received fellowship banners for gaining more than 10 per cent in new societies. After Recognition Morning, Monday next, *forty-six* States or Territories and *three* Provinces will hold these 10 per cent increase banners. Since the campaign began, two years and a half ago, *twenty-four* State unions have increased more than 20 per cent, *fourteen* have won over 30 per cent, *seven* have passed the 40 per cent mark, *four* are over 50 per cent, *two* gained more than 60 per cent, and the Hawaiian Islands lead with 116 per cent. When this campaign was proposed, that each State organize every year as many new societies as 10 per cent of the number then enrolled, few believed that a single State could keep the pace. The time-post set for the third 10 per cent is reached to-day, and *fourteen* have passed it. Ten more are almost abreast, while seven have pressed on away ahead. Numerical growth is not the most important thing, but I thank God for His inspiration of the faithful union officers that have spent their own time and their own money in organizing these many new societies.

Increase Abroad

I mention a few foreign unions only, to illustrate the marvelous advances in other lands, comparing the records of the last biennial report with those of to-day.

	1903	1905
Africa	141	224
Brazil	20	62
Bulgaria	5	15
China	188	350
Finland	7	19
Hungary	3	13
Russia	3	10
Sweden	70	148
Great Britain and Ireland	9,518	10,480
Hawaii	26	54
India	464	567

The net increase percentages figure all the way from the 10, 20, and 59 per cent gains of Great Britain, India, and Africa up to the 333 per cent increase in Hungary. And oftentimes there is work flourishing unknown. Seven societies, for example, with 500 Endeavorers were found in the Ellice Islands. In one of the Loyalty Islands there are a thousand Endeavorers out of a total island population of seven thousand, first reported this year. A letter from Ram Allah, Palestine, last month, referring to a published report, says: "You count only one society for Palestine. There are four here in Ram Allah, and I *know* of one in Jerusalem, and we hope for more."

Betterment in the States

No one can take any general look over the field of Christian Endeavor without being aware of the tremendous importance of the State organizations. Year by year they are growing in dignity and efficiency.

As a notable indication, the quiet summer vacation school or conference idea is proving valuable in State work. This past year six States have used it in one way or another.

Local-Union Increase and Betterment

A large number of local, city, county, or district unions have made earnest efforts this year to organize new societies to the extent of ten per cent. It is gratifying to record that ninety-three have succeeded. More and more small, informal conferences for careful discussion are displacing many of the large mass-meetings, while the few large rallies gain in power. Several unions conduct normal study-classes for missions, and three for a larger acquaintance with public affairs. More and more intelligence is being put into these union methods. In practical ministries, thirty-seven unions have done notable work in providing regular song services in jails, hospitals, and other institutions. Some have conducted wise and successful evangelistic services. Twenty unions report fresh-air work that is especially commendable.

Local-Society Membership Increase

The proposal that local societies try to increase 25 per cent in new members was considered a hard one. We can all join in gratulation with 1,605 societies that report this gain during the past year.

Local-Society Betterment

The report blanks this year were the most elaborate ever used, and not easy to fill out. Nevertheless, they were returned from a larger number of societies than ever before in the history of the movement; another indication of the vitality of Christian Endeavor in this year of 1905. A few months ago the societies were urged to improve their work along five lines, with the promise of special recognition for conspicuous success in any of them. It will be our delight next Monday morning to especially honor 5,406 societies for this success. The following are the points and the results: —

I. *Devotional and evangelistic endeavor.* — Here the requirement was that 75 per cent of the active members be present and participate at the meetings for six months, or to report that five or more members had joined the church, or that half the members were "Comrades of the Quiet Hour."

3,196 societies were successful in this difficult task. Altogether, the additions to the church in these societies and in the others not having the number required for recognition roll up the splendid total of 186,508 youths who have stood this year to name His name and serve His cause. There are now 37,000 "Comrades of the Quiet Hour," daily seeking the face of God and the power of His Spirit.

II. *Committee activities.* — Christian Endeavor exists for nothing if not for service. To do; to do whatever He would like to have me do, — this is our ideal and practical aim. To express in deeds the truth taught from pulpit, Sunday school, home or public school, — this is our place in the economy of the church's organization. And what a noble expression it has been this year! More than 2,000 cheering services of song in hospitals, missions, prisons, etc.! Barrels of clothing and useful articles reported from every quarter! More than a half-million gifts of flowers! Special clubs conducted for interesting and benefiting younger young people numbering 300!

We shall recognize 1,305 societies for worthy effort under this head. A few words only from the reports must suffice to indicate these loving ministries: "Started jail work. Three conversions due to personal work. Secure men employment after their discharge." "Hospital work: 3,050 bouquets of flowers, gospel sung to 3,000 persons, magazines to over 2,500 people." "200 visitations to Workhouse, Infirmary, and Old Ladies' Home." "Keep an invalid's chair to loan." "Established an employment agency for strangers." "Opened a church reading-room for young men." "Organized Industrial School for children." "Sent 84 Bibles to prisoners." "Hotel committee sends weekly sealed invitations for church services and church calendars to every hotel guest." "New hitching-posts about the church, and lights within." "Edit, publish, and distribute church paper." "Cared for large poor family all winter." "Chorus choir for Sunday evening service." "Invitations for church services distributed in boarding-houses." "Organized and support a coffee-club." "Literature-rack at depot kept full." "Regular Quiet-Hour service before morning worship in the church." "Intermediates and Juniors are especially faithful workers." "Membership contest raised us from 22 to 121." "Organized drilled military company in the society." "Made 50 scrap-books for hospital children." "Furnished boys' reading-room." "12 bouquets to the sick every Sunday, 118 glasses of jelly to Old Ladies' Home, and 20 comfort-bags to sailors." "Organized a boys' choir." "Christmas greetings to every prisoner in city jail." "Made quilts for Orphans' Home." "Ajax club for the boys." "Gathered and pressed wildflowers for Syrian day-school." Surely He who came to minister will bless the work of these loving hands.

III. Study-classes. — 982 societies report special study-classes. Of these, 927 are for the study of missions and 55 for learning more of the standards, polity, history, and affairs of the church to which they belong. This educational work is only in its beginnings. Let us magnify it many-fold.

IV. — Systematic beneficence. — 1,731 societies have been particularly good givers to the work of their church and denomination this year. First honors go again to Oxford Presbyterian, Philadelphia, which gave this year $1,554. St. Paul's Evangelical, Chicago, follows with $1,428. Among the societies giving more than $1,000 is the very first society, mother of us all, the society we all love, Williston in Portland, Maine.

Full support for some native foreign worker is provided by 125 societies. 350 specify financial aid given to their own church. The amounts given by 10,000 societies have been added up, and the sum for missions alone is $228,840.88, the largest sum so reported in the history of Christian Endeavor. The same societies report $268,960.92 given for miscellaneous causes — almost wholly for local church purposes. The roll of those who give a tenth numbers to-day 21,794.

These things are real when you read such reports as these: "Gave up a picnic planned, and sent the money to African children." "Support a colporteur's wagon in the back country of our county." "Support a native Bible reader and colporteur in China." "Formed a missionary corporation with $1 shares." Juniors "invested 10 cents per member in garden-seeds and chickens. Proceeds to missions." "Native evangelist in Tibet." "New church piano." Over and over again such lines occur. How did they do it? "Two cents a week per member for missions" is the answer of most. Will it be the answer of your society next year?

V. Christian Citizenship. — Only 46 societies have done really conspicuous work here, but their reports are gratifying: "Flower-beds on the church property planted and kept in order." "Held eleven temperance prize-speaking contests." "Closed a Sunday barber-shop." "Fought Sunday baseball." "Bought a quarter-acre of land adjoining public school; graded and improved it for the children." "Helped close gambling-den." "Resodded church lawn." "Study causes and punishments for crime in the city." "Put up a public drinking-fountain." "Stopped sale of questionable papers." "Study the city government."

So the great organization moves on with sure and firm step, guided of God as in its first fresh years.

II. — PERSONAL OBSERVATIONS

I ask your attention to a further brief statement. In a few months we shall round out the first quarter-century that Christian Endeavor has blessed the world. Standing in this twenty-fifth year, we are at the threshold of new progress in young people's work. I venture to say that the next ten years of Christian Endeavor will witness advances far wider and deeper than the last ten. Day by day the church is improving the Sunday school. We are just in the beginnings of a like devotion of intelligence to the other things that need to be done for the young of the church beside teaching them.

The coming of an assistant pastor has enabled the authorities of a Minneapolis church to revitalize and freshen its Christian Endeavor Society with glowing results. A thoughtful Nebraska minister has used his Christian Endeavor Society to devise work that has interested the whole body of the youth of the church. A New York church has had several kinds of societies for the young people, including Christian Endeavor. They are just now all being reorganized as one large Christian Endeavor Society. After a meeting of all together on a week evening, the various groups, remnants of the old societies, meet for their special business and conduct their independent plans. How much more powerful that Endeavor Society, influencing directly all the young people of the church, than the former one, merely co-ordinate with various clubs! Spiritual ends are exalted by the headship of the religious society. These churches have given real thought to the work of their young people. If these plans fail, they will give more thought, and in the end succeed. I have to report to you that this sort of careful direction is rapidly growing among the churches. This the figures cannot show. This is more significant than figures, more promising than all the splendid record revealed by the statistical report.

The more this tendency grows, the greater the need for the fellowship of a common movement. Where there is *one* strong church with able planners to take the initiative and originate plans and forms, there are *many* that have no such leadership, that are dependent on the plans of others. There is an obligation for the strong to help the weak. There is a democracy of churches as of individuals. An individual church may be snobbish even as a man. And who shall say that there is not also a democracy of denominations? What else is the fellowship of Christian Endeavor?

Christian Endeavor is not yet done with this fellowship idea. There is a better democracy among the young of that New York State church just mentioned than when there were various organizations. Other churches, too, must solve the problem of bringing together those of superior attraction and greater privilege with the less privileged or less gifted.

When the great men framed the Constitution of the United States, they based its provisions on confidence in the voice of the people. To be undemocratic is not to care for the voice of the people, not to be interested in the other man's opinion. Forever and ever Christian Endeavor is against that attitude. It wants the educated youth of every church to know and to care what the thought of the less privileged is. It wants the weak church to touch the strong for the good of both. It is greatly aiding to bring to an end the days of foolish sectarian misunderstandings. We cannot justly expect peace among the nations so long as there is ill will among denominations. A living American patriot said the other day that the United States should be a gentleman among the nations. Our country will play so noble a part only as we shall preserve and enlarge true fellowship among the young, and true democracy among the churches.

Life is glorious. It is good to be young to-day. Let us not be behind our times. Let us know our country, and study her welfare. Let us believe in the church, and eagerly uphold her honor and her labors. And while we ask the church to be thoughtful for the youth to-day, we may not forget that even to-morrow we shall be that older membership charged to turn and help on those that will follow us.

With these true, strong words, American and Christian to the core, the Report and the first session came to a close, after the benediction by Rev. Samuel McNaugher, of Boston. It was a great session, successfully carried on against odds. All knew now that the Convention was going with power.

CHAPTER II

The Praise of the Nations

AT THE ARMORY, WEDNESDAY NIGHT

A UNIQUE session in the history of Christian Endeavor conventions in this country was this. For the first time, but not for the last, most certainly, an entire evening was given to a service of song. And such a song service! It was rightly named an International Festival of Praise by Rev. Carey Bonner, of England, who arranged and in large part composed it. Mr. Bonner has done much to raise the musical standards among the young people in England, and by this praise festival he has given a wonderful impetus toward a higher class of music in America. The whole occasion was remarkable, and raised enthusiasm and delight to the highest point.

What a spectacle it is to see a crowd gather! From seven o'clock on the people began to come in a steady stream. Badges, badges everywhere, with the splendid Baltimore Convention badge conspicuous. Never have we had so elaborate and beautiful a badge as this. At eight o'clock the Armory is filled, crowded. Not a seat is unoccupied, and standing room cannot be found for more, although thousands outside want to get in. A sea of faces, a vast motion of fans, a tense air of expectancy. All the elements of inspiration are present. Not less than eighteen thousand, probably more — all the daily papers said twenty thousand — delegates and friends of Endeavor were ready to hear such sacred music as they had never heard before.

There were some preliminaries. One of them was a surprise especially designed by the chairman of the decoration committee. While the crowd was settling into place some hymns were sung, and then it was announced that the hall would be darkened for a moment, while — Suddenly the electric lights went out, and the vast amphitheater was in darkness. As suddenly an arch of incandescent lights shone out above the choir. Amid the outburst of applause, on the left of the rear wall appeared, outlined by electric bulbs, the shield of Baltimore, bearing the Battle Monument in the center. A moment later, on the right blazed forth Maryland's coat of arms in colored bulbs. Next came the Baltimore badge, above the organ, with its exquisite lines. Then that monogram "C. E." which is recognized around the globe, shone in dazzling brilliancy from the center of the organ. By this time it seemed as though the thunders of applause would raise even that stable iron-girded roof. But there was the climax of all when, across

IN THE ARMORY

the broad organ front the Christian Endeavor motto, "The World for Christ," in letters of golden light two feet high, on a background of red, illuminated the choir and platform. Applause and cheers, long continued, witnessed the effect of this ingenious use of electricity for noble ends. Already a sermon had been preached — civic and state, national and international righteousness, and world-wide evangelism — a sermon glowing with the gospel light — an electric epistle read of all. Superb preparation for a superlative service.

It was in this surcharged atmosphere that the following telegram to Dr. Clark was presented to the body by Mr. Shaw, whose voice was found to have the most carrying power of all the speakers as yet, save the Governor: —

BALTIMORE, July 5.

DR. F. E. CLARK, *Pine Point, Me.*

Fifteen thousand Christian Endeavorers from many lands send sympathy and love, and pray for your speedy and complete recovery. We pledge anew loyalty to Christ, fidelity to his church, and fellowship with his people. The greatest meeting in the history of our conventions.

(Signed) H. B. GROSE,
For the Convention.

"All who favor sending this, say 'This for me,'" said Mr. Shaw, repeating it until the response thundered out so loud that it seemed as though Dr. Clark, listening, might almost have heard it.

Dr. James L. Hill, veteran Endeavorer, who presided, introduced Mr. Bonner. "The greatest of all meetings in our radiant history," said he; "a meeting that will begin a new era of vocal music in Christian Endeavor." He extolled the musical genius of Mr. Bonner, saying that the Christian Endeavorers of the world stood at his feet in London at the Festival of Praise in that city, and that they should do the same here. Mr. Bonner was a natural leader, an original man, and he was not only able to do, but was capable of inspiring others with his beautiful music. He had made his name as a music maker, and had printed his name in the annals of music. Dr. Hill then showered high praise upon the immense chorus that had been gathered for the Convention, and said that it was the most magnificent ever assembled. The chorus manifested great appreciation of this tribute, and so did the audience.

Dr. Hill then introduced Mr. Bonner, who came forward on the platform and bowed to the great audience. In a well-modulated voice, and with a pronounced accent on every word, he thanked Dr. Hill and his comrades in the Convention for their appreciation of the music, and added: "Great Britain greets her sisters and brothers of America in the praise of God, and we now shall join in the festival of praise. I ask that all enter into the spirit of the occasion with the greatest devotion."

He bowed to the audience, and with baton in hand turned to the choir, the members of which again greeted him with the waving of handkerchiefs, the sight presented being a most effective one. A more beautiful scene, indeed, it would be difficult to imagine. Two thousand singers, grouped in three divisions, with a hundred children, little girls whom it will not injure to compliment for their lovely faces, in the forefront. The vast majority of that choir ladies, all in white. No wonder the audience found it difficult to heed the leader's injunction that, as this was a religious praise service, there should be no applause, but only reverent hearing; no wonder that before the service was over the pent-up feeling should find vent. It was simply impossible to keep it in. In the responsive readings and congregational hymns the thousands who had the musical score united. The whole effect was majestic, overpowering, spiritualizing. No session of any convention anywhere ever made deeper impression for good. No words can do it justice. We try to give an idea of the service, by this mere outline, conscious of the impossibility of conveying the effect.*

The service was opened by the quartet and choir, who sang the Sanctus in E, "Holy, holy, holy," by John Cambidge, doctor of music and organist, of York Minster, England. The choir and congregation joined in William Kethe's paraphrase of Psalm C, to "The Old Hundredth," originally published in Day's Psalter in 1550. The Lord's Prayer was sung by the choir, the people sitting. This was followed by a responsive reading from the Bible, with prayer refrain by the choir,

"I am listening, Lord, for thee;
What hast thou to say to me?"

The Aaronic Blessing was sung in unison by male voices, and repeated by the full choir to one of the oldest of the Hebrew melodies, it being claimed that it was sung by Hebrew priests in the journey through the wilderness of Sinai. The congregation and choir sang the Hebrew hymn, "The God of Abraham praise," to the Hebrew music "Leoni," named after a great singer in the Duke Street Synagogue, London.

Next was a contralto recitative and solo composed by Mr. Bonner to the words "When I survey the wondrous cross." This led up to the chorus from Mendelssohn's oratorio St. Paul, "How lovely are the messengers," by the whole choir. Part second followed, presenting the response to the evangel in the praise of the Church Redeemed. It opened with soprano solo, "I hear ten thousand voices singing." A response by the quartet followed. "Praise ye the Lord, for He has given to lands in darkness his light."

China's praises were sung in a typical native Chinese air, composed entirely on the five-tone or pentatonic scale. The words were written and the music harmonized by Mr. Bonner. The peculiar melody was very effectively sung. India's praise was represented by two Bengalee songs, translated by Dr. William Carey. The song No. 11, entitled "Endeavor Band," was very remarkable, both in melody and rhythm, utterly unlike any sacred music heard in Europe or America. It was in eight verses, without the slightest musical variation. The Bengalee hymn, "O my soul, do not forget Him," was written by Krishna Pal, the first convert baptized at Serampore. It is now a favorite hymn at oriental communion services. The praises of Africa were illustrated by two compositions well known in America, entitled "Turn back Pharoah's army," and "We shall walk through the valley."

The praises of Great Britain were given in the words of the old hymn written by Edward Perronet, a helper of John Wesley. The words were set to the tune

---

* This "Festival of Praise" has been published by the United Society of Christian Endeavor and can be secured for 25 cents a copy, which includes both the words and music, or 10 cents a copy for the word edition only.

called "Diadem," composed by James Ellor, of Lancashire, and which has become a great favorite with British Endeavor choruses.

The praises of America were expressed by the words of Dr. Roy Palmer's hymn, "My faith looks up to Thee," the music by Lowell Mason, in the tune "Olivet." Silent prayer was followed by short scripture responses, and the children's choir sang Jemima Luke's beautiful hymn, "I think when I read that sweet story of old." The venerable authoress, living now in retirement at Newport, Isle of Wight, sent a message of greeting to the children of America, with her portrait.

Part third expressed the response of the Evangel in the praises of the church glorified. No. 19 began with a tenor solo, "Give me the Wings of Faith," music by Mr. Bonner, which introduced the chorus from Handel's "Messiah," "Worthy is the Lamb." No. 20 was the Watts hymn, "Come, let us join our cheerful songs," music by Dr. Croft. This hymn led up to the great Handel chorus, "Hallelujah." The service closed with the Mizpah benediction, composed by Mr. Bonner — "The Lord watch between me and thee when we are absent one from another."

One of the sweetest of the choruses was that of the children, "I think when I read that sweet story of old." As the rapt faces of the children were seen, intently watching their leader who held them as in a spell, the audience burst into applause that told how hard repression had been. Masterly, masterly — the hand of a master musician was felt in it all.

The vast audience dispersed quietly, still under the spell of the music. There was but one feeling about it, that it was a new feature to be continued, provided the musical leadership could be obtained. Surely it can be, for America has capable leaders, although none with Mr. Bonner's peculiar personality.

So the first great day of a great Convention — surpassing in that evening audience any single gathering even Christian Endeavor ever knew before — came to its close. "Baltimore — 1905" was stamped with a brilliant and superlative success.

How Mr. Bonner Leads

From a singularly able characterization, made by some unknown writer in the *American*, we give this picture of the leader. It is entitled, "How Carey Bonner Leads."

"It is not so much what Carey Bonner can do," said one of the speakers last night, "but what he can inspire"; and his words were fulfilled when Mr. Bonner arose and after a short greeting to the vast multitude swung his baton in a graceful curve about his head and, with teeth clenched as if about to enter a great battle, nodded his head to the organist and the battle was on. When the last Hallelujah was sung and the people crowded around the bashful genius and showered him with congratulations, they looked at his slight figure and his easy smile and said one to another, "How can he do it?"

If one watches Mr. Bonner carefully during the entire performance he may still be very much at loss as to just how he does it, but a slight inkling comes once in a great while which tells something of the wonderful magnetism of the man and the power of his genius.

No one can sit and look at the swing of Mr. Bonner's baton who will not in an instant wish that he could sing. There is something about that curve of the long, white stick and the force behind it which impels his hearers with a desire to sing, to help him out. He seems to be in some dilemma, and he is working so hard to get out of it. His whole body will sway with the baton as it swings in a circle about his head or makes a downward flight toward the floor. The listener knows that Mr. Bonner is trying to make him sing, and how he wishes that he could help. The baton describes another circle, and the audience feels the thrill of impulse.

As a trainer speaks continuously to his beasts, so does Mr. Bonner keep up a running flow of talk to his singers. His lips move and the singers know that he is beseeching them to pay strict attention to the score; a hard passage is being neared and a corner of his brown mustache is drawn slowly into his mouth and he chews on it hard as the passage draws nearer and nearer. It passes and the mustache is liberated, and on the face of the director, which is mobile in a degree throughout, there creeps a smile, and the people in the armory sit and listen and say to one another, "How does he do it?" It is the mouth that tells his story; the struggle that he undergoes every time he directs them is reflected there. It is a tale of suffering which the observer sees on his face throughout the performance, brightened at rare intervals by that smile of content as his people glide over a passage smoothly.

With the older members of the choir his baton is a log of heavy wood. He is dragging the music from their throats as if by main strength; but with the children all is different. Softly and easily he starts his baton with its sweep. Once it circles around his head and then, looking intently into their faces, he says softly, "Now, now, now, now," and the last one is as soft as the first, but the children are gazing at his face as if their immortal salvation rested upon their look. Their eyes are never taken from his face, and so swiftly does he turn from one to another that every little girl feels she knows that he is looking into her face and is asking her to sing. He is not caring for the others, he is asking "her" to sing, only her, and she is doing all in her power. It was like a choir of innocents last night to hear their tones, and as inspired by the genius of the slight man with the baton the song of the Christians arose and painted to the hearers a picture of those days when Christianity was practised by stealth and the church was the plaything of the heathen kings. The chorus swells and softens to a caress. The song is ended, and the audience, with their eyes upon the leader, draw a deep breath and say one to another, "How does he do it?"

CHAPTER III

Endeavor in Meditation

THE QUIET HOURS

WHAT a variety the Convention program presents. Something surely for everybody. In place of the long favored sunrise prayer-meeting has come the Quiet Hour, followed by the School of Methods — a natural passage from meditation to service.

The Quiet Hours at Baltimore had exceptional leaders. The place, the Associate Congregational Church, was delightful for such a meeting, and was crowded with devout Endeavorers. At the first meeting, Thursday morning at eight, Dr. Robert A. Hume, the eminent missionary to India, and a former president of the India Union, brought a special blessing to every one present as he gave his imaginary conversation with a heathen Hindu on "How to become acquainted with God." The same method might well be employed with Christians. The address is in every way remarkable, reflecting the peculiar personality of the speaker.

"I have only two hands, and all my greetings by hand-shakings with all men must be done with those hands; only two eyes, and all I see must come through those eyes. So my heart has hands and eyes, and all my acquaintanceship, with either God or man, must come in the same way." Then he went on to tell his Hindu friend how men become acquainted with one another, as by writing letters, by sending messengers, by talking with one another, by silent influence upon others' thoughts, by living with one another, and how in all these ways men get acquainted with God.

President King, of Oberlin College, treated the same great theme on Friday morning. He spoke, with the manly straightforwardness for which he is famous, about human friendships, their value, their sanctity. They depend, he showed, upon mutual self-revelation, mutual self-surrender, and community of interest. Now God asks of us, for our friendship with Him, no more than what we ask of our human friends; only, there are necessary flaws in human friendships, arising from the limitations of human character and knowledge, but our friendship with God may be perfect, with no misunderstandings or withholdings.

Miss E. Stafford Millar, the Australian evangelist, is a lady with a wonderfully eloquent and interesting face. The theme of her Quiet Hour service was "Be ye filled with the Spirit." She told of some

Christians who were testifying. One said that the well of his Christian experience had been fluctuating, sometimes high and sometimes low, but on the whole about three-fourths full. Another said that his had for fifteen years maintained a steady level, about three-fourths full. Then a third spoke up: "If that well for fifteen years has never been emptied and then filled up full again, it must be half full of wiggle-tails." How to become filled with the Spirit, and how to make use of the power and blessing He will bring, — that was the great message she brought to us from the Antipodes.

These Quiet Hour services grew constantly in interest and attendance, and they taxed to the utmost the capacity of the large church in which they were held. Their influence upon life and character cannot be measured.

CHAPTER IV

Endeavor at Work

SCHOOL OF METHODS: CONFERENCES AND STUDY CLASSES

ONE of the busiest hours of the Convention days was that from nine to ten — the hour devoted to what is called the Christian Endeavor School of Methods. This included Mission Study Classes, Bible Readings, Conferences of Pastors and Junior and Intermediate Workers, Christian Culture Conferences, and Conferences on Endeavor Methods and Personal Work. Many found it difficult to choose between so many good things, but whatever the selection there was no lack of interest. Perhaps the largest attendance was upon the Endeavor Methods and the Junior Workers, but the attendance generally was excellent — it was nothing less than surprising when it is known that the spell of weather continued, with humidity, heat, and frequent tremendous rainfalls, so that physical endurance was severely tried.

CHRISTIAN ENDEAVOR METHODS

This conference was led the first morning — Thursday — by Mr. Shaw, and as all knew that he knew about all that is worth knowing about these methods, there was a crowd that filled the Associate Congregational Church to the doors. There was a different leader and topic for each day, and the first was "Christian Endeavor Spiritual," treated with reference to securing new active members, improving the prayer-meeting, winning the young people to Christ and the church, and deepening the devotional life of the young people. Mr. Shaw, the leader, declared that he had never before attended a meeting in which the Endeavorers took part so magnificently.

The second morning dealt with "Christian Endeavor Practical," considering the improvement of committee work; doing more for the Juniors and Intermediates; helping the young people along social, literary, musical, and athletic lines; and the place of clubs for boys and girls. The leader was California's vigorous field-secretary, Rev. E. H. Hadlock, Ph.D.

The theme for the last meeting was "Christian Endeavor Advancing" along the different lines of the Society in the large church; in the country; rural family Endeavor; the solution of various problems of leadership, education, etc.; and individual consecration. Mr. John R. Clements, the able secretary of the New York State Union, was the practical leader.

With such subjects and live leaders there was a rapid fire of questions, answers, reports, suggestions, and experiences, and any earnest worker could soon have filled his note-book with ideas well worth trying, and enough to last him for many months.

The Pastors' Conferences

These meetings of the pastors to talk over ways and means, and get light as to better and best ways and means, were exceedingly helpful and interesting. They were in the hands of three skilled leaders, President Stewart of Auburn Seminary, Secretary Vogt, who is a master at conferences of this kind, and Dr. Biederwolf, the evangelist whose power to reach men reminds one of Moody in his earlier days.

There was an earnest and large company of ministers in the Central Presbyterian Church each morning. Dr. Stewart led them in consideration of such themes as the kind of organization needed for village and country churches, over- and under-organization, the pastor's relation to his organizations, and other important themes. At one point in the discussions Dr. Stewart asked the pastors what kind of societies they should have in their churches. He found that many seemed to think they should have precisely the kind of society outlined in the Model Constitution. But one pastor answered, "We should have just the kind of society we need." "Precisely!" asserted President Stewart; "as Lincoln said of the proper length for a man's legs, — just long enough to reach the ground."

Secretary Vogt led the conference on Friday morning. The ministers discussed the reasons for young people's societies, the use and misuse of the pledge, associated clubs, and other practical topics. Many questions were asked, and Secretary Vogt's answers were particularly helpful in making perfectly clear the position of the United Society on certain important questions, and the full liberty given the pastors to mold their societies to fit the need of their churches. The Trustees had declared their position emphatically on this point.

The conference led by Dr. Biederwolf discussed the all-important matter of evangelism. It was a privilege that the ministers enjoyed to hear this eminently successful evangelist, be stirred by him to the importance of evangelistic work in their churches, and get from him many practical hints as to the best methods. Dr. Biederwolf, while of course he did not in the least minimize the essential work of the Holy Spirit, yet was wisely insistent on the truth that no amount of filling with the Spirit will take the place of a knowledge of the best ways of reaching men, and energy in carrying out those plans. Here are some of his pithy sentences: —

> It needs no superior insight to assert that the demand of the hour is for an Evangelistic church. The church of God has been victorious just in so far as she

has been evangelistic; this has been and always will be the secret of her power. A church that is not evangelistic owes the world an apology for its existence.

The church to be evangelistic must be pure in doctrine, faithful in discipline, democratic in spirit, philanthropic. But when all this has been said, it must still further be an aggressive, up-to-date church. Max Muller has said "the church must be aggressive or cease to exist." Christianity should be marching and conquering, and not simply holding her own behind ecclesiastical embattlement. The name of Eggleston's church in "The Hoosier Schoolmaster" is richly suggestive. He called it the church of the Best Lick. Brethren, we must not search the camp for a champion — this is not a David and Goliath affair. The victory we so much covet is not to be won by some knight of the cross pricking forth alone in search of adventure — not by stately evangelist or the lordly minister, but by the church as an organized army in which all shall be at it and at it all the time. There are too many members in our churches who are living in the 23d Psalm, where it says, "Lord, make me to lie down." It's very hard to get some members to do anything — to try it is like trying to drag a cat backwards by the tail over the carpet, but there are whole hosts of them who would willingly work if the work were simply given them to do. I have even heard of a pastor who said when his members offered their services, "I know of no work to be done," but a real minister would never be guilty of a thing like that, and I suppose if those members had suggested some undertaking for the kingdom he would have been like the minister who had never learned to harness a horse, but the time came when he had to do it; he threw the harness down on the floor and tried to drive the horse into it. It is true of the real pastor, as some one has said, "If he were that dragon fly with 35,000 eyes he could not see all there is to do; if he were Briareus with 100 arms he could not reach the myriad extremities of human needs about him," yet his motto ought to be, "Never do anything yourself you can get anybody else to do," and when the thing presents itself he will know how to do it or give himself to a diligent acquaintance with church methods that shall help him to a thorough mastery of the situation in manipulating the multifarious forces about him.

Home Mission Study Class

This was in charge of Don O. Shelton, widely known among the young people as Associate Secretary of the Congregational Home Missionary Society, and a most enthusiastic teacher and worker. Several hundred of the Endeavorers gathered each morning to study with him some of the home mission heroes, following the method of his text-book, "Heroes of the Cross in America," with use of a syllabus. He took up Brainerd and Whitman and what the home missionaries have done for the Northwest, with a special study on America's greatest need — the overwhelming appeal of home mission work. In the course of this study he said: —

It is apparent that the more thoroughly America is Christianized, the more speedily the whole world will be evangelized. Our obligation to do our utmost to evangelize the whole world does not exempt us from responsibility for the thorough evangelization of America. Neither does the presence of duty near at hand free us from the utmost possible exertion in behalf of distant nations. The substance of the divine command is, Forward the whole Christian army for conquest at home and abroad!

Therefore, the study of home missions, as well as of foreign, will have a place in the program of every wisely directed missionary committee.

Scarcely any study is more fascinating or profitable than that of the workings of God in American history and of the present moral and spiritual welfare of our nation.

Through an intelligent study of home missions will come a knowledge of what God has already wrought in America. His guiding hand will be recognized in many of the processes by which the nation has become what it is.

Even our greatest historians have failed to describe the far-reaching effectiveness of the work of the pioneer preachers of the gospel.

American historians, for the most part, have dwelt on the secondary rather than on the primary causes of the nation's greatness. The home missionaries braved no less severe sufferings, made no less heroic sacrifices, and were no less truly winners of the West than their distinguished contemporaries whose lives were spent in warring and in politics. The equipment of every young man and woman should include a knowledge of the heroic and fruitful labors of these stalwart men, who, in their life and work, aimed to do the will of God by founding a Christian nation.

Foreign Mission Study Class

Equally fortunate were those who came to the study of methods under the direction of Mr. Harry Wade Hicks, the young people's secretary of the American Board for Foreign Missions. Thorough knowledge of the subject and the way to make it interesting enabled him to be helpful to all who attended his meetings. He used a full syllabus on the work of missionary study classes, local missionary committees, and union missionary committees. The class which was organized became an object lesson, and learned how to do by doing. Sample text-books were introduced, and different ones who had made use of them told of the results. Everything was done to keep to the level of actual service and training, in which the leader is an expert.

The discussion was directed along lines suggested by questions in the syllabus. Some of these were: "If the foreign-missionary society of your denomination has rendered aid, how did it do so, and of what value was the service?" "How may leaders of classes be fitted to lead?" "If you were urging a person not familiar with foreign missions to enter a class, what reasons would you give?" "How may young people be given a wide and intimate acquaintance with foreign missionaries and the leaders of denominational missionary work?" "How may the regular monthly meetings of city or local unions be utilized to promote interest in foreign missions?"

The balance between theory and practice was kept throughout. Questions were asked calling for the statement of general conclusions. When an answer was given, the one offering it was promptly asked to illustrate it by some actual experience, and thus the meetings were made of the most practical value to workers.

Conferences on Personal Work

There are a great number of Christians who want to do something for the Master but do not know how, especially when it comes to the vital matter of personal effort in soul winning. Out of this need grew the conferences led by Mr. C. C. Michener, of the International Committee of Young Men's Christian Associations, and Rev. C. L. Evarts, of Boston, an evangelist, who has a special gift in the use of the Bible with the unconverted and with seekers, and a system which will enable any one to acquire facility in such use of the Word as may help inquirers and strengthen saints alike.

Practical and specific directions were given as to the best methods of study and of work. Helpful literature was recommended, Dr. Johnston's "Studies for Personal Workers" being given a foremost place. The possibilities of such work were illustrated by abundant experiences. The method of having a small group of workers gradually brought together in a church was suggested as most valuable, and especial stress was laid on the importance of keeping the matter entirely secret. Doing the work, not talking about it, is the essential point.

Numerous queries and difficulties were presented, and were answered by citing cases from personal experience. The interest often caused the discussions to overrun the time, and the leader was sought for further advice after the meetings were dismissed.

Christian Culture Conferences

Miss Margaret Koch has a constantly widening acquaintance among the Endeavorers, and inspires all who come within the circle of her conferences with love of the Bible and appreciation of its beauty and meaning when properly read; also with a just regard for the body, which needs to be trained for Christian service and made the medium of strong and noble life. Physical and voice culture were her themes, broadly divided. She finely illustrates in her own personality the subjects of which she treats entertainingly. In one conference she called attention to the way in which we miss much of the most familiar psasages of Scripture simply because of their familiarity, so that the words are repeated in parrot-like fashion with little thought of the meaning. A brief study of the twenty-third Psalm was made in illustration of the point, because that is one of the parts of the Bible that suffers most in the way mentioned. The audience was asked to repeat the Psalm together, especially for the purpose of dwelling on its images, and some of these were illuminated by helpful comment. As to reading the Bible effectively, she said: —

In order to read the Bible so that it will mean something to those listening, there must be a real desire to read it in spirit and truth. The next step is to really get the meaning of the passage and live with the thought of it until one gets a feeling from it, then the expression will take care of itself, providing that the agents of expression, the body and the voice, are free so that they will express the thoughts one feels.

Regarding the influence of the body on our work for Christ she said: —

The real ego is never seen, only as it is manifested through the body. In order that the Christ-spirit may be manifested in all its power it is necessary to cultivate the body so that the two will be in harmony, so that the Christian may indeed be "known and read of all men."

No positive rule can be given saying you must practise a certain system of physical culture, and that then you will be able to do better work for Christ, but a general principle can be laid down, to the effect that whatever exercises are practised must be taken with a view to making the body more radiant and responsive to whatever thought we wish to express. Since we learn more through the sight than the hearing, it is very important that the body should express thought as well as the voice. When a speaker's body says, "I believe every word I am saying," he does much stronger work than when the body is unresponsive, merely standing there — a piece of cold clay.

The voice is like a many-toned instrument. Not all people appreciate the same kind of music. So the voice must be attuned to express any and all kinds of thought. The Book of Books contains all kinds of emotion, which must be expressed. If the voice can only express one thing we cannot do effective work for the Master. The voice must be so cultivated that it will express all the varied emotions that are needed to reach the people for Christ.

The Junior Conferences

The Junior conferences were held each morning at Trinity Methodist Episcopal Church, and there was on hand a strong body of Junior workers to lead them and carry them on. Mrs. Clark was to have been one of the leaders, and in her enforced absence with Dr. Clark her place was taken by Mrs. James L. Hill, former superintendent of the Massachusetts Junior Union. A letter of deep regret for her necessary absence was received from Mrs. Clark, and the gathering sent her a message of loving sympathy.

Mrs. Hill and Rev. Geo. H. Kenngott, of Lowell, Mass., both widely known in Junior work, made capital directors of these conferences, and the ever-ready Junior workers took part with vivacity and wisdom. Miss Haus presented the subject of Junior prayer-meetings. Miss Olney, of Rhode Island, spoke of the inculcation of kindness to animals. Mrs. Hodgdon, of St. Louis, treated the Intermediate society. Miss Grace Jones, the New York Junior superintendent, talked about the littlest Juniors. Mr. Kenngott on the first morning gave an especially valuable address on missionary literature and charts, and other helps for missionary study by the Juniors. Miss Haus talked about church membership for children. Most of the many practical topics were discussed in fresh, spontaneous, impromptu fashion, question and answer flashing back and forth in glorious eagerness.

At the conclusion of the first session the workers repaired to the basement of the church, where Rev. Mr. Kenngott gave a further lesson in Junior work by an exhibition of methods used successfully by himself in Massachusetts. Rev. Mr. Kenngott possesses one of the finest collections of charts for this class of Endeavor work in existence, and the greater part of his collection was brought to Baltimore to be placed on exhibition for the education of others who are engaged in the same work.

In the same busy Junior headquarters on Thursday afternoon, a reception was given to all Junior superintendents and other workers in Junior societies. The rooms were crowded with many scores of interested Endeavorers. Nearly every State in the Union was represented. Mrs. Suter, Maryland's earnest Junior superintendent, with Miss Post, the successful president of the Baltimore Junior Union, were busy everywhere promoting sociability. Refreshments were served, many helpful acquaintances were formed, and the occasion will long bear fruit for the Junior movement.

The most important action taken by the Junior and Intermediate workers was the organization of an International Union of Junior and Intermediate superintendents, the purposes being to promote the advancement and broaden the influence of the Junior associations by means of closer fellowship among the workers. The union will include superintendents of national, as well of State and local societies. The following officers were elected: —

President, Rev. George F. Kenngott, of Lowell, Mass., superintendent of Massachusetts Union.
Vice-President, Mrs. Antoinette Suter, Junior Superintendent of Maryland.
Secretary, Miss Kate Haus, of St. Louis, Field Secretary for Missouri.
Treasurer, Miss Nellie Williams, Cherry, Col.

These officers, with three others to be selected by them, will form the executive committee. The constitution of the organization provides for biennial meetings at the time of the international convention of the general organization.

Professor Duxbury's Readings

The Endeavorers were eager to hear Professor John Duxbury, of Manchester College, England. His Scripture recitals in many parts of our country had aroused much interest in the talented elocutionist and inspiring scholar of the Bible.

The series, which was given in the imposing Gothic edifice, the Mt. Vernon Place Methodist Episcopal Church, began with a specialty of Professor Duxbury's, the recital of the book of Job; selections from the life of Moses and from Paradise Lost were given on other days. So great was the interest in the book of Job, which is made to live in the mind of the hearer, that the ministers of Baltimore prevailed upon the obliging and genial master of his art to repeat it for their especial benefit. This he did on Monday morning, to a crowded house. The delighted hearers passed this resolution: —

Resolved, That we express to Prof. John Duxbury our hearty appreciation for his admirable recitals and bid him godspeed in his journey across the sea.

Professor Duxbury is quiet, dramatic, and wonderfully effective. He feels so deeply that he makes his hearers feel, without extravagant efforts on his part, the power and beauty of the Bible. Thus he is dramatic in the best sense of the word. Those that listened to him gained a new conception of the way to make the Word of God strong and vital in the lives of listeners. He was greatly delighted with his reception in Baltimore and in America, and expects to return in the autumn for another visit.

Conference of State and Local Union Officers

This was an exceedingly spirited meeting, held in the Associate Congregational Church. Secretary Vogt was in charge, with able lieutenants in Treasurer Shaw and Dr. Hallenbeck, president of the New York State Union, and one of the very much alive and progressive executives.

Notwithstanding the fact that the rain was pouring in torrents at the time the conference convened, the church was crowded to the doors with the state presidents, secretaries, and treasurers.

Mr. Vogt was the first speaker, and he talked for a few minutes on the importance of unions and that it was necessary for the life of the unions to be strong.

Miss Antoinette P. Jones, of Falmouth, Mass., corresponding secretary for the Floating Christian Endeavor and the World's Christian Endeavor Union, spoke for a few minutes. Her work is among the sailors and soldiers and the crews of all kinds of vessels, and she gave a very interesting talk regarding her work. She was not scheduled to speak, so Mr. Vogt gave her the preference of having the floor first.

The first topic was "The Federation of Unions." Rev. Elliot Field, field secretary of the New York State Christian Endeavor Union, asked what was meant by the federation of unions. Mr. Vogt then went on to explain that the main object in planning the federation was to provide a union work secretary who would be constantly in the office at the service of the unions, to aid them in securing speakers, to study their knotty problems, help them exchange ideas, plan new union organizations, and strengthen the efficiency of all Christian Endeavor unions.

Mr. Shaw was called upon by Mr. Vogt to explain to the conference the Dr. Francis E. Clark memorial fund. In outlining the larger endowment plan, Mr. Shaw explained that this greater proposal would provide, among other things, the resources for such a union federation secretary.

Dr. E. H. Hallenbeck, president of the New York State Union, of Binghamton, N. Y., introduced an informal motion endorsing the testimonial fund as outlined by Mr. Shaw. Then followed a scene of great enthusiasm, every State in the conference seconding the motion at one time, with Indiana in the lead and Ohio following. It was decided that the motion was unanimously carried.

The next topic was "Independent Unions," and Mr. Vogt was also asked to explain this. The topic called forth considerable discussion from the floor, and each State made a report about the condition in their cities. It appears that in some of the cities Christian Endeavor unions have joined with the Epworth League and Baptist Young People's Union. The delegates reported that in all such cases the union has been anything but satisfactory. Mr. Vogt pointed out that neither the United Society nor the State unions could keep in touch with societies through independent local unions, whose officers might not be Endeavorers. He urged the importance of pure Christian Endeavor unions.

CHAPTER V

For the Boys and Girls

THURSDAY was field day for the Juniors. They held forth in the Armory morning and afternoon. That is, the morning session was for and about them, and the afternoon session was just them, in flesh and blood. It was the greatest Junior Day by far in Endeavor annals, and that Rally will go down as one of the shining features that made this the Superlative Convention.

The morning session, at 10.30, could scarcely have been held under more disadvantageous circumstances. The rain fell, and when it was not swiftly falling it threatened to, and the oppressive heat continued. In spite of everything, however, there were five or six thousand Endeavorers on hand, and they entered into the spirit of a splendid session with a fervor that not even the necessity to raise an umbrella here and there where the Armory roof sprang a leak could subdue. President Stewart presided in his happy vein, keeping things going. Mr. Jacobs led the hymns, and the choir had a right to a morning off after the severe exertion and superb singing of the evening before. The devotions were led by Dr. Ralph W. Brokaw, of Utica, one of the original Trustees, who has been lightly touched by time and keeps the buoyancy of the earliest days of the great movement.

President Stewart introduced the first speaker as the "plain and great William Shaw — without any degrees: Some people grow less, by degrees." Treasurer Shaw gave a vigorous review of what Christian Endeavor has done in the last quarter century, and if any man knows it he does, for he has been actively engaged in the work since 1885 at Old Orchard. He is original in pretty much everything — original trustee, original treasurer, original business manager, original speaker, with a wonderful voice that will keep any audience awake and listening. Here are some of the good things he said: —

A missionary, returning to this country after an absence of many years, was asked what feature of church life impressed him most. He replied instantly, "The wonderful activity of the young people in church work." The changed conditions in our church life have come about so gradually that many people have failed to note them. We judge by comparisons.

Twenty-five years ago the ruling idea in the church was that children should be seen and not heard. The result was that few were seen and none were heard.

Twenty-five years of Christian Endeavor have revealed to the church that it is out of the young people that the Kingdom of Heaven is to be made.

This week 66,000 Christian Endeavor prayer-meetings will be held, and tens of thousands more by societies that belong, and ought to be, in our fellowship.

A PORTION OF THE AUDIENCE IN THE ARMORY

These prayer-meetings are the class-rooms of the churches' spiritual training school. Here the educational principle, "No impression without expression," is being worked out.

In perfectly natural ways young people are given an opportunity to give expression to their aspirations and ideals, and to cultivate their talent as witnesses for Christ. The possibilities of these services along evangelistic lines cannot be overestimated. Here, under the most helpful conditions, young people are faced with the question of decision for Christ, and here, surrounded by their companions and friends, they receive the training necessary for growth in character and service.

In our plan of Junior, Intermediate, and Young People's Societies, with the Mothers' or Parents' Society added, we have a system that is scientifically correct and practically workable. Its degree of efficiency depends upon the leadership and material furnished by the local church.

Twenty-five years ago the church that had a well-organized young people's society was the exception. To-day the church that does not have such a society is a curiosity.

Christian Endeavor made the prayer-meeting the heart of the movement and has laid great emphasis on testimony and prayer, as it ought; for without prayer and testimony the church would die. The martyrs and confessors rank together. In the history of great deeds the voice "crying in the wilderness" has always preceded the deed.

But Christian Endeavor has not only a heart and voice, but hands and feet as well. Through its system of committee work it offers opportunity for training in service to every member. This training is as broad and comprehensive as the mission of the church, and covers every department of life and activity.

It recognizes the religious, social, and intellectual needs of the young people and the claims of philanthropy and reform. The system is so flexible that it can be adapted to the needs of the smallest, or the requirements of the largest church. It unifies the activities of the young people, so that while each department is in charge of specialists all are united in the common work.

Through the executive committee it gives to the pastor a cabinet by which he can touch and direct every line of work in which the young people are engaged.

Twenty-five years ago a small percentage of the churches had mission circles composed of girls or young ladies. Now we have thousands of our brightest and best young men vying with the young ladies in their interest and enthusiasm for missions. Tens of thousands of missionary committees are at work, and thousands of mission-study classes are conducted.

Last year the gifts of the young people to missions reported to the Presbyterian General Assembly amounted to $184,000, and this is a sample of the new missionary asset that has been developed.

Less than 10,000 societies reporting to the United Society the actual amounts contributed for beneficence for a period of five years gave a total of $2,187,000. Not a penny of this was given to the United Society or used in Christian Endeavor work, but every dollar was a contribution to the missionary and philanthropic work of the church.

And yet once in a while we read a criticism of Christian Endeavorers, because in addition to their gifts to other causes they give a small sum to strengthen the movement in their own Local or State Union, or through the World's Union to the mission fields afar. I venture the assertion that there is no organization in the church that has given so much, or that has enlisted so many unpaid workers in the service of the church, as the Society of Christian Endeavor.

Twenty-five years ago the young people's paper was a goody-goody child's story-paper, and the young people's department in the church papers consisted of a weak storyette. To-day our young people's papers are the peers of any publications, strong, aggressive, virile, practical, spiritual, and successful.

Twenty-five years ago a young people's religious convention was unknown; now they rank as the largest religious gatherings of our time, and exercise a commanding influence in the public life of our day. They challenge the attention of believer and unbeliever alike, and are striking manifestations of the vitality of the young people's faith.

Twenty-five years ago the young people of the nations and denominations were isolated and unknown to each other. Now, with no loss of loyalty or fidelity to their own nation and denomination, they are united in a world-wide brotherhood, exalting him who is King of Kings and Lord of Lords.

These strong statements concerning the work of Christian Endeavor were heartily applauded, and the cheery spirit of the session was established.

The second speaker was our beloved devotional leader and devoted Junior worker, Dr. Floyd W. Tomkins of Philadelphia, whose topic was, "What More shall we Do?" He said in part: —

There is a great deal of work to be done as far as bringing young people into the church is concerned, and it must be done immediately if the church of God is to have the power it has longed and looked for. There are four things that I wish to present to the delegates assembled here.

First, young people should be drawn more closely to the church, and the only way to accomplish this is to bring them into the Christian Endeavor Society and not go outside of the church and indulge in general work. A great failing is that few ministers attend their Endeavor meetings and spread that spiritual influence that is necessary. Every minister, in my opinion, should go to all the Endeavor meetings in their church and stay through them. Preach to the children and bring them into the church and place them in the pews, where they can hear everything, and then talk to them so that they can comprehend what you are saying.

Secondly, we want a closer union in the work of Christ. The children do the work far better and with more enthusiasm than the older members. We must do all we can towards educating the young people of to-day. There are large numbers of young people to-day who will drink. There should be a campaign of abstinence. When we succeed in defeating the drink evil we will be able to down the saloons. If beer will rot away the leather on the boots of the saloon-keepers, what will it do to the stomach of an ordinary mortal?

Thirdly, we must teach young people purity — purity of thought and purity of deed. We must teach them the higher ideals. There should be a campaign against divorce. A child in Newport met another child, and pointing out a man that was walking down the street, said, "There goes my father." "Oh, pshaw," replied the boy addressed, "that's nothing. He was my father long ago."

The children should be taught honesty, and not to accept one cent that has not been honestly earned. They should be taught not to accept tainted money and give it to the church, for if they do the church will never be brought to a high standard of morality.

Fourthly, lead the children up to the service of God. Teach them to become Christians, and not tell them what they are to be when they grow up — doctors, lawyers, or what not. Teach them that, and in twenty-five years what will be the result? There will be a vision hardly recognizable. Teach them above all purity, temperance, Christianity, and fidelity to duty, and they will become nobler beings and fit to associate with the highest in the land.

Rev. Albert Swift, of London, president of the London Christian Endeavor Union, spoke on "How the Pastor Can Help." He said every minister should be a strategist. A pastor accomplishes the most by giving his attention to the children, for there he has a work that will lead to eternity. If the minister does his work and brings the children of to-day into the church he will have those who will be the men and women of the church in the future. If we want to win the children we must teach them the beauty of the gospel, and we should teach these little folks in the meetings of the church. They have no appreciation of the forms of the church, so they should be taught simple things within their comprehension.

"Every Endeavorer must be a minute-man, sometimes a fifteen-minute-man," said Dr. Stewart, introducing Dr. William T. McElveen, of Boston, who replaced Dr. Luther Deyoe, of Pennsylvania. He spoke on "How the Home Can Help." Always ready and witty, he related a story about his son, which created considerable laughter, and brought out a point he wanted to indelibly impress upon the juniors. He sent his son to a German kindergarten in New York, but there he did not acquire much knowledge. When he reached Boston he entered the boy in a school of a different kind. The boy had not been studying long before he returned home and told his father that he knew how to spell and that he could spell in English.

"How do you spell 'boy'?" asked Dr. McElveen of his son.

"M-a-n," replied the little fellow, with a toss of his head, as if he was proud of his ability to spell the word. The father was amused, and instantly thought the method of spelling in Boston was the new-fangled one he had heard of.

"Well, then, how do you spell 'man,' my son?" was the next query.

"You spell it the same way, only with capital letters," replied the boy.

"Now, my friends, that is the point I want to illustrate. The Juniors are small, but they should spell their name in big letters. It should be the task of the home and the function of the Christian Endeavorers to spell their natures in big letters."

Miss Kate H. Haus, of St. Louis, field secretary of that State, was the first woman to appear on the platform as a speaker. Her topic was "The Call for Superintendents." She had a penetrating voice, and defied the rain more effectively than some of the men, gaining great applause. She said in part, in her keen and epigrammatic style: —

The need must be met or we are not fulfilling God's command of Deut. iv. 1, 2, 9. The fall of Eve showed the value Satan put upon childhood. He wanted Eve's children.

The lives of Abraham, Moses, Samuel, David, Daniel, and the three Hebrew children show the value of child training. Pharaoh's conduct in Ex. x. shows how he valued children. To-day we profess to value them, but we neglect them, as results show. God valued childhood by having Jesus, the Saviour, begin his life a babe.

If we follow Jesus we must value childhood by obeying Christ's command to "Feed my Lambs!" The basis of our obedience is love. "Lovest thou me? Feed my lambs!"

While we have been busy with self, with plans and methods and peace conferences and congresses, Satan has been busy training the children on the streets, in saloons, cheap shows, through cards, cigarettes, and the evils of society.

We can't get the men of to-day because we did not train the boy of the past. The Endeavorers are not doing their full duty in not caring more vigorously for the Juniors.

In Matthew xviii. we find we can "offend the child" by neglecting to train him for Christ. The popular excuses for not having a Junior society are like gasoline — quickly evaporate under God's gaze. We can find ways and means to establish a Junior society — if we wish to do so. We will be held responsible by God for our negligence in this respect.

"Lovest thou me? Feed my lambs!" We lack the love for Christ that constrains to action. If we love Christ we will keep His commandments.

The Armory was a rather desperate place for an Open Parliament, but Rev. C. H. Hubbell, of Columbus, Ohio, field secretary of the State that produces presidents, is a brave man as well as splendid executive, and did his best, repeating the answers given. He called for testimonies as to what the Juniors have done; and how the testimonies rushed in! "They have made me know more about God." "They have shown us how to take part more promptly in our meetings." "Our Juniors take part in the Senior consecration meetings." "They teach us how to do a willing service" — "how to give" — "how to study our Bibles" — "how to join the church." "They teach us simplicity and earnestness." "Our Senior society has been saved by the Juniors." That is the way the testimonies came in; and while our hearts were warm with them, Mr. Hubbell led in a resolution service that meant real resolves to go to work for the children.

All the delegates bowed their heads in silent prayer for the spread of the work of the Juniors. While they were in this attitude of devotion, Dr. W. H. McMillan, of Allegheny, Pa., led in prayer, and Dr. De Witt M. Benham, pastor of Central Presbyterian Church, Baltimore, followed with the benediction.

A VIEW OF THE CEILING DECORATIONS

A NEAR VIEW OF THE CHORUS

CHAPTER VI

A Superlative Junior Rally

A WONDERFUL, UNFORGETABLE SESSION

THAT Junior Rally, with its song story! Were you there? Then you will never forget it, though you live into the next century. Let us all hope that we may hear others as thrilling and moving; but it will be a difficult thing for anybody to accomplish. The standard has been set up close to the skyline, and the Baltimore Junior Chorus of fifteen hundred voices takes its place in Endeavor history among the unapproachables.

How the elements conspired against the children and the occasion for which months of preparation and the most careful training had been spent by Leader Porter and his choral regiment. Between two and three o'clock, the appointed hour for the great meeting, the clouds let themselves loose again, and down in sheets came the rain. But the anticipation had been too great, and mothers wrapped up their children and went forth with them. Before the hour the Armory was filled, just as it was the night before, only now nearly half the immense multitude was composed of lads and lassies, all in white. The rear gallery was full of children, and looked like a vast bank of white flowers, specked by the yellow and black fans bearing the C. E. monogram. But the choir galleries — what a sight they presented! Shall we ever see another such on earth? Such beautiful faces and so many of them, looking like great flocks of Raphael's angels escaped from paradise and come down to bless the old earth for a little while. They were bubbling over with pleasure and excitement and jubilation, for now the event had come! They were to be the center of attraction, and indeed they were. The scene made all the much-used adjectives, even the superlatives, slink away into obscurity, as trivial and unfit for the occasion. Let us say simply that it was profoundly soul stirring to sit and look at that choir, then clear across at the thousands more of boys and girls in the gallery, and reflect upon the possibilities of power for good wrapped up in those little lives. To think, too, that here they were having put upon them the touch of Christian Endeavor, of service, of sacred song, of holy influences — getting a start toward the true and worthy things in life. Much as the Juniors affected the audience of older ones, quite as much the Convention will influence them. That Rally could not fail to leave a lasting impress upon the youthful minds and hearts.

Thoughts like this ran through the mind of the onlooker before that chorus sang. When it sang the impression became too deep for words. Amid all the rising and overflowing enthusiasm of that hour, there were times when you could see tears in many eyes, brought there through the medium of sacred song as those thrilling young voices, sweet with the melodies of the spheres, sent it forth. The editor of the *Christian Endeavor World* rightly says that "after the magnificent praise service of Wednesday evening it seemed that any other musical session must prove but an anti-climax." It seemed so, but there was no anti-climax. All were carried higher and higher. Indeed, as "The Story of Christian Endeavor in Song" was told by the chorus, under direction of its skilful leader — Mr. H. W. Porter (who composed the greater part of the music, the words being written by two Baltimore Endeavorers, Miss Emma Post and Miss Nellie A. Davidson), the spirited music was rendered with a precision, distinctness, and finish not surpassed by the older chorus the evening before. And the richness and harmony of the fresh voices, many of them touching the thrill line that runs along the spinal cord, went straight to the center of the soul.

The musical exercise was long and the day was oppressively hot, but the director held the children steadily to their work for more than an hour. The Juniors entered with vim into every part of the service, and had plenty of spirits left and plenty of voice, as they showed by the repeated outbursts of shrill applause and cheers which only awaited half a chance. So there grew a feeling of cameraderie between chorus and vast audience, and they cheered each other back and forth with uncontrolled glee and enjoyment. The Juniors not only put the most into it, but for reward they clearly got the most out of it. It should be said that applause was not forbidden at this service. That was fortunate, because no rules would have been obeyed when enthusiasm became so contagious. It started in early, even at the sight of the Armory and the chorus, and lasted till long after the session closed, venting itself in the song that rolled out into the streets and the cars as it had not done before. The Junior Rally was the Senior Rousement, as the preacher would put it. Taking the two choirs together, the familiar letters "C. E." must now stand another significance. When we think of Baltimore we shall say, Choral Effectiveness and Charming Ever, which may be added to "Best Yet."

It is difficult to keep the eyes off the singers long enough to get this remarkable session open, but it must be done. When order was brought out of the chaos of settling in place, hymns being sung meanwhile under lead of Mr. Foster, Professor Grose announced that as Dr. Landrith, who was to have presided, had been drafted for the evening session, the presiding officer would be one of the best friends the Juniors ever had, Dr. Hill, who was greeted as he deserved to be. Devotions were led by Rev. Alexander Esler, of Canada. Then all was ready for the cantata, for which a special program had been distributed. As number after number was given the audience listened with positive delight, which manifested itself at every pause.

Beginning with a song of Welcome, the second number was "Christian Endeavor! the name beloved in every land," sung to Gounod's music. "Suffer the Children to Come" followed, an exquisite piece. "Junior Christian Endeavor" told how the little ones, in the Master's name, "in the ranks of C. E. do many deeds, loving deeds." Then came one of the most touching and effective sermons in song ever preached, and preached to one of the greatest congregations ever gathered. It was called a Choral Duet. There were two great sections of the chorus, one soprano, the other alto, and they sang back and forth the invitation of the Master, "Come unto me, all ye that labor and are heavy laden, and I will give you rest." The first division ended with, "Come! Come!" four times repeated, and what a plea it was as the young voices sounded it forth. Then the second division took up the refrain and sang "Take my yoke upon you," ending with the same appealing "Come!" Both sections now united, and repeated the entire verses, the close repeating that word "Come!" eight times, with marvelous sweetness. Tears sprang to the eyes, and all hearts were moved. There was an instant's silence, and then the applause continued insistently until the chorus had to be repeated. Emotion and enthusiasm commingled swept the great throng, and the children caught the magnetism and responded joyously. Other hymns were rendered, and then the "Missionary" hymn, which introduced a sub-chorus of Juniors dressed to represent the different races and nations. This was exceedingly well done, and formed an object lesson that delighted an audience already roused to a high pitch.

Now rest came for the singers while Miss Grace Beelman, of Ohio, cornetist, played one of the gospel hymns with such spirit of devotion breathing through the silver-toned instrument as made an encore inevitable. She caught the entire company when, in response, she played "Maryland, my Maryland," and the chairman could do nothing until she appeared again. This time she started "Nearer, my God to Thee," and a vast volume of song arose as all joined in the hymn loved of all Christians.

The Life Preserver

If ever a speaker had an audience prepared for him, Rev. C. H. Tyndall, of New York, had this one. And he filled well his place, with his object-lesson on the good and the unsafe life-preserver. He had two, which looked exactly like those found on steamboats. He belted one on, and then proceeded to show what it was made of. Each section was hollow, with a little door, and he took out the varied contents, remarking on each.

Many ships leave Baltimore every week for all parts of the world. They all go prepared for storms and accidents. Each one carries life-preservers.

This is the way they look (displaying a large one), and this is the way they are put on. They are supposed to be filled with cork or something else which will float the heaviest person. Each voyager in life has some kind of life-preserver on which he depends for the time of need.

Some of these are very disappointing. Here is one of that kind. You see it has doors to the compartments, and I propose to turn inspector and let you see what is inside. I open the door of the first compartment and discover a beer bottle and a wine glass. Whether in joy or sorrow, some people depend upon alcoholic liquors to help them. They are poor life-preservers. You see I also find a serpent in this compartment. This is ever a companion of the wineglass. "At last it biteth like a serpent, and stingeth like an adder." Wine is a mocker in the time of trouble and at all other times. Have nothing to do with it.

In the next compartment I find a Sunday newspaper and a trashy novel. Those who spend their time storing their minds with such things have nothing else to help them in the time of trouble. Be careful what you read.

In the next compartment I find wood, hay, and stubble. These are worthless things. You are gathering into your lives what you will need in time to come. Form habits of pure thinking, earnest study, and hard work.

A small balloon is in the next compartment. It represents the bubble of pleasure for which some young people live. You strive very hard to get it, but no sooner do you touch it than it is gone. (Touching the balloon, it explodes.)

In the other compartment is something upon which many people depend. You see it is a chain of gold and silver. Money is valuable, but it is a poor thing to have as a help in sorrow and death. And yet there are those who work so hard for it that they fasten upon themselves the habit of love for money, which is nothing less than a chain of gold and silver which weighs down their soul.

Thank God, there are life-preservers which are not so deceptive. The other one which I have represents the kind that every true Christian has in the time of need. Let us inspect this also.

In the first compartment I find a Bible. The Word of God is like a solid rock under one's feet when he feels himself sinking. Heaven and earth shall pass away, but the promises contained in this book shall never fail.

In the next compartment I find a map of that greatest city on earth — London. If you were put down in that city, this would tell you just where to go. The Christian has a map of the heavenly city in his life-preserver. I find here also a compass. Its needle always points toward the north, and on the darkest sea it would tell you which way to take. If we belong to Christ, we have such a compass. It is the voice of God saying, "This is the way, walk ye in it."

In another part I find a telescope. That brings distant objects near.

In another compartment I find a large document called a passport.

Rev. R. A. Hume, D.D.

Rev. Albert Swift

Mrs. Mary Wood-Allen, M.D.

Miss Kate Haus

Miss Margaret Koch

Miss E. Stafford Millar

It is signed by the Secretary of State of this great nation. It describes me, and says that I am a citizen of the United States, and that I may freely travel in foreign lands, and am to be protected. If you are a Christian, you have a passport. It declares that you belong to the heavenly country; that you are to be protected while down here, and that you are to be freely admitted into the heavenly city.

In this life-preserver is also a candle. This is for the time of darkness. If you believe in Christ, however dark it may be, "then shall your light break forth as the morning, and the glory of the Lord shall be your reward." You see, I but touch this candle with this glass rod and instantly the candle springs into light.

But in the last part of this life-preserver we have something which includes everything else. What could we do if we did not have the Holy Spirit to live in our hearts?

We think of the Holy Spirit as being like a dove, because he so came upon Christ at his baptism in the Jordan; and perhaps because he is gentle, beautiful, loving, swift, and pure. He is our divine helper, living in our hearts until the body returns to the dust, and then he takes us with him to the heavenly home. That helper in the time of need is represented by this beautiful dove which I find in the other compartment of this life-preserver. One has said: —

> The dove let loose in eastern skies, returning fondly home,
> Ne'er stoops to earth her wing, nor flies where idle warblers roam.
>
> Sweet Bird of life! Celestial Dove!
>   I knew not what a gentle guest,
> Fresh from the heart and hand of love,
>   Had lodged within my aching breast.
>
> Beneath that Dove's encircling wings,
>   My struggling spirit broke her shell;
> Escaped from earth and earthly things,
>   In fairer, brighter worlds to dwell.

As Mr. Tyndall let the dove fly from his hand, it soared away into the great space and finally lighted on one of the iron roof girders. This caught the Juniors and they cheered him with a will, waving their fans in the air, while the audience joined. It was a telling exercise, and the temperance and other good points were vociferously applauded.

Secretary Vogt had a most welcome message and his voice rang out strong and clear as he gave it. He read a telegram from President and Mrs. Clark to the Junior Endeavorers, which was greeted with cheers, and sixteen thousand handkerchiefs were waved again in the Chautauqua salute. Here it is: —

Affectionate greetings to all Junior Christian Endeavorers. "Be ye therefore followers of Christ, as dear children." MR. AND MRS. FRANCIS E. CLARK.

Secretary Vogt asked authority to send greeting to the Epworth League Convention, now in session at Denver, and the following message was dispatched: —

EPWORTH LEAGUE CONVENTION, *Denver, Col.:*

The International Christian Endeavor Convention, at Baltimore, reaches hearty hands across the continent to greet the Epworth League at Denver. "One is our Master, even Christ. We are all brethren."

Dr. Hill announced that, in response to a request, Miss Ellen Stone, whose captivity several years ago was a matter of international interest, had consented to make them a short address. Miss Stone came forward and was greeted with the heartiest applause. She first spoke to the children in the chorus, who cheered her and waved their fans at her.

"It was for you that I said yes," she said, "when I was asked to come and speak to you, because I have been so delighted to hear your songs for Jesus and know that you are working for all that is good and noble." Then, turning to the audience, she said: "Dear friends, the word must be first for the children, then just a little to congratulate you who are training them in the principles and work of Christian Endeavor." A like warm greeting came from the thousands.

Then Dr. Hill drew great applause from all, and especially from the Juniors, when he declared that this Convention would be signalized by the fact that it was a convention of great audiences never before equaled. This outshone in brilliancy, too, any that had preceded. It was a convention, he said, of distinguishing features — a great musical convention — and that it would give an impetus to sacred song. "There is no other city on this planet," he said, "that could produce the music by Juniors that you have heard this afternoon. This achievement will embarrass the cities that will follow you in any attempt they may make to equal it." How the chorus caught that up, and cheered again and again.

THE FLAG EXERCISE

It might have been supposed that the end of this record-breaking rally had been reached, but the climax of wild enthusiasm was now to come. The "Flag Exercise" proved to be one of the most ingenious and brilliant numbers imaginable in its brilliant scenic and musical effects, and took the audience by surprise, even after the other surprises. The effect cannot adequately be described. This exercise put this Junior Rally on a pinnacle by itself. At a signal by the conductor the great division on the right became, in the twinkling of an eye, a great flag. Every girl and boy, quick as flash, produced a cape and cap, throwing the cape over the shoulders and the cap on the head. Some capes and caps were red, some white, some blue. When the change was made, there appeared the white stars on the blue ground, in the corner, and there were the white and red stripes, so that the human, flag was perfect. As "Star Spangled Banner" was sung the little bodies swayed to and fro, giving the flag a waving motion exactly to the life. This was too much. The singing was drowned in cheers. The audience rose and waved handkerchiefs and cheered with delight. The second and third divisions of the chorus joined in applauding their mates. The singers joined in, and the scene was complete.

Now another signal, and a similar transformation took place on the left. The hundreds there whipped out black and yellow caps and capes and donned them before the slow eye comprehended what was taking place. Then they struck into "Maryland, my Maryland," only the words were Miss Harker's, and religious in sentiment: —

> File into rank for Christ to-day,
>   O Maryland, dear Maryland.
> Free to the breeze His banners play,
>   Maryland, dear Maryland.
> Your noblest work for Him be done,
> From early dawn till setting sun,
> Nor cease, till latest victory's won,
>   Maryland, my Maryland.
>
> CHORUS.
>
> Shout, shout for joy the glad refrain,
>   Maryland, my Maryland.
> Our King shall claim his own again,
>   Maryland, my Maryland.
>
> "Christ and His church," your watchword be,
>   Maryland, dear Maryland.
> Till time becomes eternity,
>   Maryland, dear Maryland.
> His Gospel spread through all the land,
> His heralds, each Endeavor band,
> And may they make a gallant stand,
>   For Maryland; dear Maryland.

Again the song was interrupted by an enthusiasm that could not be restrained. What could come next? There was the central great division. Nation and State had been represented, what was left? A third time the leader gave that magic signal, and as instantly, without a miss by a single maid or lad, caps and capes of white and red appeared, forming the "C. E." in the white and red of Endeavor. Again the cheers rolled forth, even before it was possible for the singing to begin. A semblance of quiet restored, the "Christian Endeavor Flag Song" was sung. Flags were now added to the caps and capes, and all three divisions united in the great chorus, waving the flags in unison with the music. The sight was one of the prettiest conceivable, and sight and song together were simply thrilling, captivating, irresistible. Here are the words: —

CHRISTIAN ENDEAVOR FLAG SONG

> A flag loved and honored by many brave hearts
>   We find in each nation unfurled;
> But one flag is honored and loved in all lands,
>   And claims as its home all the world.
> Wherever the far-reaching light of our Cause
>   Is shed over land, over sea,
> There hearts true and loyal are thrilled by the sight
>   Of the sign of our glorious C. E.

CHORUS.

> For Christ and the Church it inspires us,
> To do and to dare and to be;
> And long may it live in all nations,
> The sign of our glorious C. E.
>
> O God! for the light it has spread through the world,
> The lives it inspires us to live;
> The service to Thee, to Thy Church, and to man
> It leads us and helps us to give;
> For the fellowship drawing all nations as one,
> And binding them closer to Thee,
> We thank Thee! we bless Thee! we praise Thee, O God,
> For the gift of our glorious C. E.

Now audience and chorus vied in salutes and applause. The audience cheered and gave the Chautauqua salute, and the chorus cheered back and waved the flags frantically; then all cheered and waved together, until finally some one started "My country, 'tis of thee," and the vast throng dispersed, singing itself forth into the streets of Baltimore. Had the Convention ended then it would have been remarkable enough to have warranted use of all the adjectives. One enthusiastic Endeavorer, a veteran convention goer, voiced a general sentiment when he said, "I never expect to hear such singing again this side of heaven, nor to see such a spectacle." The standard has been set by the Baltimore Junior Rally of 1905. All the Junior leaders felt that their work had received a mighty impetus.

THE JUNIOR CHOIR

Mrs. James L. Hill has kindly given this fine tribute to the Junior Choir: "A better trained choir of boys and girls cannot even be imagined. Their music reminded one of a composite photograph. The time was so perfect that it seemed as if there were but one singer, yet the volume of sound and the blending together of various individual qualities could not have been obtained without the thousand little voices that helped to make the beautiful tone-picture, and many people think that the very acme of this most musical Convention was reached in the rendering by the Juniors of the incomparable song, 'Come unto me and I will give you rest.' This favorite text, sung without any paraphrasing and with strong, rich, churchly music, seemed like a direct invitation and promise from the Master himself, and when the final words, 'Come, Come,' were rendered softly, yearningly, and pleadingly, it seemed as if all the Juniors of that great choir were making a thousand personal urgent appeals to the audience to accept the blessed invitation."

CHAPTER VII

The Brotherhood of Christian Endeavor

AT THE ARMORY

Two great meetings were arranged for the evening. At the Armory the world-wide brotherhood of Endeavor was recognized. It was a field service, and another object lesson of striking character. There had been the usual downpour of rain just before the hour of beginning, and the size of the audience did not equal that of the afternoon, yet it was a great audience, more than twelve thousand, and the interest did not flag. Things were kept moving with despatch and good feeling by the ready presiding officer of the evening, Dr. Ira Landrith, whose sallies were well received. The speakers did uncommonly well in making themselves heard, although they had to yell. The international fellowship idea has never been more ably presented or more interestingly. It was a cosmopolitan program indeed. The Scripture reading was by an Englishman, Professor Duxbury, who recited the parable of the prodigal son. Prayer was offered by Rev. I. N. D. Gordon, of Jamaica. Then there were twelve brief and pointed addresses by representatives from China, Japan, India, Porto Rico, Macedonia, Jamaica, England and Canada, the American Indians and the Negroes. The audience gave most hearty greeting to all, and the speakers were inspired by their reception. One of the most taking features of the service was the singing of a native air by the sisters from India who are being educated in this country. Modest and attractive, with sweet and low voices, their quaint melody made its way to the heart, and they were encored.

The first speaker was Bishop Walters, of the African Zion Methodist Episcopal Church, an honored Trustee of the United Society for many years, and a man of great native eloquence. He congratulated the Endeavorers of Baltimore, very tactfully and gracefully, on the catholicity of their spirit in permitting negroes to enter the Convention and sit side by side with the white delegates without an objection. He had been in the audience, and had seen many others of his people present, but had not seen a single look or heard a word that would indicate any distinction of race or color. He declared that this was a unique recognition of brotherhood, and made an impassioned appeal for the help of the Endeavorers in lifting his race to the highest level of Christian civilization. The audience cheered him to the echo, and an equally cordial greeting was given to Bishop Arnett, of the African Methodist Episcopal Church, — "that black man with a white heart," as Dr. Landrith called him.

"Will there be any stars in my crown?" was sung with splendid effect by Rev. F. H. Jacobs, who, with Mr. Harris and Mr. Foster, made up an unsurpassed trio of Convention musical directors. The audience wanted to hear him again, but Dr. Landrith said they had to go all the way around the world, and could not stop for another song.

A full-blooded American Indian spoke next, representing the many Indian Christian Endeavor societies. He was Mr. Stephen Jones, recently elected traveling secretary of the Y. M. C. A. His earnest words were followed by the first greeting from the five Christian Endeavor societies of Porto Rico, "that island which we have recently, more or less benevolently, expanded around," as Dr. Landrith said to the merriment of the quickly responsive audience. This greeting was finely brought by Rev. J. A. McAllister, who said that seven years ago the Bible was forbidden in Porto Rico, but now there are seventy-three churches and seven thousand members, and the people are learning to be Christian Americans — the greatest thing in the world. Another near-by island was splendidly represented by Mr. John E. Randall and Rev. Edward J. Hewett, secretary and president of the Jamaican Endeavor Union, with its two hundred and fifty societies and almost twelve thousand members.

After a charming rendition of an anthem by the chorus, we continued our trip around the world, leaping to China, to which we were conducted by a missionary from the Flowery Kingdom, Rev. Henry G. C. Hallock, Ph.D. — "evidently a Presbyterian missionary," remarked Dr. Landrith, as Dr. Hallock came forward attired in a beautiful blue Chinese costume, queue and all. "Over in China," said he, "we are boycotting American goods, all but Christian Endeavor. In that we have doubled our supply the past year." He continued: —

It gives me great pleasure to be here at the great "Best Yet" Convention, and to bring these greetings from China. Five years ago Dr. Clark traveled ten thousand miles to bring your greetings to China and to encourage us in the great work there. We appreciated his sacrifice in coming. He kept his eyes open and saw one of our needs and through kind friends was enabled to supply it. It was a national secretary, in the person of Rev. George Hinman, and we are grateful not only for the generosity, but because that generosity has been fruitful in China. Mr. Hinman has been a hard worker, a faithful traveler, and a prolific writer of Endeavor literature in Chinese. He has been successful also in getting a number of scholarly writers in Chinese to write much in Christian Endeavor lines, but, best of all, his work has resulted in the organization of many Christian Endeavor societies in Manchuria, in coast cities, in Yang-tse Valley cities and in interior cities.

"We're just going to take a Knipp at Japan," said the bright chairman, and Rev. J. Edgar Knipp swung the audience with him as he waved the banner of the sunrise empire. There was no doubt as to the sympathies of his audience. He said: —

I bring you most hearty greetings from the Endeavorers of Japan, the "Land of the Rising Sun," the land of hope, the land of the future, the land of Nogi, Oyama, and Togo. The courage and the perseverance that made these mighty warriors victorious in their recent battles are characteristic of the young Japanese Endeavorers in their battles for our King, Jesus Christ.

AN ARMORY AUDIENCE, FROM THE REAR GALLERY

We believe that the war in the Far East now going on between righteousness and unrighteousness, between the army of Christ and the army of the evil one, is a greater conflict than that just drawing to a close between Russia and Japan. And yet, as true Endeavorers, our hearts are filled with hope, for we know that He whom we follow has gone forth conquering and to conquer.

Although comparatively few in number, our 2,800 members, belonging to 126 societies, are scattered from the Hokkaido, on the north, to Formosa, on the south. We believe, therefore, that as the leaven gradually permeates the whole lump, so these groups of Christian young people will grow in number and, influence throughout the country.

We rejoice that so many young people in America are reading and studying the little book, "Sunrise in the Sunrise Kingdom," for we believe that as your knowledge of the Christian work in Japan increases, your prayers in its behalf will become more frequent and more fervent and you will add to the petition "God save America for the sake of the world" the kindred one, "God save Japan for the sake of the nations of Asia."

Rev. Jiro Abratani was also to have spoken for Japan, but did not appear. Dr. Landrith thought the Czar would be glad to hear the news, — "One Jap lost."

Rev. Alexander Esler, one of the Canadian trustees, spoke eloquent greetings for his country, and by that time Mr. Abratani appeared from the meeting in the Lyric. He was received with great enthusiasm, and brought his nation's greetings in excellent English, urging upon us Togo's watchword for the fleet in his great battle, "Do your utmost."

Rev. F. S. Hatch appeared in complete white attire, Hindu fashion, to speak for the India where he labored three years for Christian Endeavor. He introduced two charming Indian Christian Endeavor maidens, Miss Ethel Meriam Maya Das and Miss Dora Mohinie Maya Das. The latter told the audience how there were eighty Endeavor girls among the one hundred scholars of the school where she was educated, and something of their work; then she and her sister sung very sweetly an Indian song with Indian words. Dr. Hume also spoke for this fifth country in Christian Endeavor, and for the second largest society in the world, his own great body of Endeavorers in Ahmednagar numbering five hundred and twenty-eight. He paid highest tribute to Endeavor for the help it had been to the missionaries in their work. He bade us "put it down in every book, 'Calcutta for 1909.'"

Rev. Albert Swift spoke for "the old country," and the ties that bind America and England were united the more closely by the greetings he bore from his own land, and from his own great London Union, which he had just learned to be the largest in the world. He declared he would go home holding his head higher.

It was especially suitable that the World's Convention, to be held next summer in Geneva, Switzerland, should be announced at the close of this stirring session. This pleasing task was performed in a most wide-awake way by Mr. Lathrop, and those that go to Geneva will find there personal representatives from nearly all of our world-wide brotherhood.

Everybody felt that it was the close of a great day at the Armory — the second day of a memorable Convention that was rapidly making history.

CHAPTER VIII

The World-wide Brotherhood

AT LYRIC HALL

BROTHERHOOD was the keynote of the meeting in Lyric Hall also. This charming place, charming because one could hear and because it was a relief to go from the vast audiences to the more family-like atmosphere, was crowded to overflowing. Evidently the tour around the world which Mr. Graff promised to make with his audience had been a magnet, as it should be. He has gotten together a remarkable collection of slides, bestowing an immense amount of time upon the work, and also knows how to tell the picture story of Endeavor. Nobody made a mistake in going to Lyric Hall, and all there seemed to appreciate to the full their good fortune. The exquisitely colored views, showing Christian Endeavor domiciled in every clime, drew forth constant applause.

But this is getting ahead of the evening's order, as laid down in the program. The electrical effects were admired, as were those in the Armory, and the colors of the decorations were exceedingly harmonious and pleasing to the eye. The ceiling of the vestibule was hidden by evergreen, giving refreshing suggestions of the woods. Among the masses of green and along the pillars and ceiling of the main hall shone red, blue and green electric lights. American flags were draped from the gallery, and also convention and state badges. Streamers were suspended from the center of the ceiling, reaching to every corner in the auditorium. Tiny electric lights were concealed within vari-colored paper coverings, and the light thrown out was weird and soft. The stage was decorated with palms and cut flowers.

President Stewart, of Auburn Seminary, one of the brightest of the presiding Trustees — and what a lot of brilliant men Endeavor has in its service — hastened to say that he was not "he of the 57 varieties," Mr. H. J. Heinze, who had been expected to preside. But there was no lack of relishes and spice in the exercises.

A portion of the large choir — probably four hundred voices — occupied seats in front of the stage. The music, which was rendered beautifully, was led by Mr. Percy S. Foster, of Washington.

The meeting was opened with a praise service that lasted ten minutes, after which devotions followed, led by Rev. Dr. Allan B. Phillputt, of Indianapolis, Ind. "Voices from Across the Seas," was the next on the program. The first speaker was Rev. Dr. Hallock, of China, who, garbed in the native costume of the Chinaman, told of the work of the Christian Endeavor Society in the Far East, and what good it was accomplishing. He caught the audience at the start by shaking hands with himself, which is the Chinese form of salutation. He related many humorous narratives about China, and concluded his remarks by thanking the United Society for sending to the missionaries in China thousands of dollars with which to carry on their work.

Mr. C. Ogawa, of Japan, followed Dr. Hallock, and when he stepped upon the platform he was greeted with prolonged applause. He briefly told of the spread of the Society in Japan, and how Christianity had performed wonders in the Land of the Rising Sun. He said there was no religion on earth like Christianity. His message, reiterated and emphasized, was, "If the world is to be saved, it must be saved through Christianity, for Christianity is the only religion that saves people." As he closed a "Banzai!" for Japan and for Christian Endeavor was shouted from the gallery, and the audience cheered.

Miss Evanka S. Akrabova, of Philippopolis, Bulgaria, was the next speaker. She said that her country was only two years older than the Christian Endeavor Society, as twenty-seven years ago it was freed from the yoke of Turkey. In her country, she said, the Christian Endeavor movement is being carried on in a wonderful way. She told a story of an Austrian lady whom she met after she had returned from a trip to America. The lady, she said, told her that America was a land of vanquished impossibilities, and she heartily concurred with her. With a tribute to Secretary Hay as a true Christian Endeavorer, she told Bulgaria's need for just the kind of citizens that represent President Roosevelt's ideal for America. "Only the golden rule of Christ will bring the golden age of man" was her closing sentiment, which was loudly approved.

Rev. Dr. F. S. Hatch, formerly secretary of the Society in India, was then welcomed, and after interesting remarks he introduced Misses Ethel Meriam and Dora Mohinie Maya Das, of India, who he said would sing several songs in their sweet voices. The sisters sang the first song, which was a native one, in the language in which it was written. While they were singing in their rich, dulcet tones the vast audience remained unusually silent, and the words could be distinctly heard in the farthest corner of the auditorium. When they had finished, their performance was greeted with applause, and they were compelled to sing another hymn. This was selected from the Endeavor Hymnal and was "Abide with Me."

The section of the Convention chorus sung with great effect an anthem under the leadership of the Convention organist, Mr. Robert L. Haslup, whose popularity won him a rousing reception.

Then came the stereopticon lecture, which the *Christian Endeavor World* thus summarizes: —

> We had seen the living representatives of many lands. They had appealed

to us in behalf of their native countries. We could not hope to visit in reality the homes of all, but the next best thing was made possible within a brief space in the special feature of the session, the stereopticon tour of the Christian Endeavor world presented in one hundred and fifty fine views, Mr. George B. Graff being the admirable guide. The journey started with Williston parsonage on the evening when Christian Endeavor was born. The hour was spent in a remarkable unfolding, not only of the world-wide extension of the movement, but of the almost innumerable developments that have proved its adaptability to widely varying conditions. The massing of details and the appeal to the eye were most impressive, even for the hearer most familiar with the past history and the present work of Christian Endeavor. Prison societies, societies among life-savers, a society of veterans in a soldiers' home with members averaging sixty-five years of age, a society among lepers in Dutch Guiana, were among those that figured on the screen. A fine group of Floating Endeavorers on a war-vessel was heartily greeted. A visit was paid to the Christian Endeavor Seaman's Home at Nagasaki, Japan.

We saw the church in Alaska that grew out of a Christian Endeavor society's tent, and saw the tent maintained as a relief station on a glacier where many lives have been imperiled. There were pictured drinking-fountains erected by United States Endeavorers, and the fine fountain set up by Winnipeg Endeavorers as a memorial of Queen Victoria's jubilee.

We looked on the faces of societies and individual workers in China, India, Turkey, Ceylon, Egypt, Palestine, South Africa, Spain, Wales, and the islands of the sea. Conventions in America, Japan, India, London, and elsewhere showed a strong family resemblance. There were bits of the home life and the methods of travel in different countries, illustrating conditions to be faced. Glimpses of unusual methods were shown, like the group ready to start with a stereopticon to tell the gospel story to their heathen neighbors.

The tour closed with a look at the Boston headquarters of the Society and at the portrait of the founder surrounded by some of the workers.

This closed a session of remarkable interest and information. The story of Endeavor, with the aid of the appeal to the eye, was made more impressive than words alone could ever make it. No one who saw and heard the Picture Story will doubt the world-wideness of Christian Endeavor.

Rt. Rev. Samuel Fallows, D.D., LL.D.   Rev. Washington Gladden, D.D

Rev. George F. Kenngott   Rev. J. Edgar Knipp

Rev. Charles Stelzle   Prof. John Duxbury

CHAPTER IX

Rally Day, State and Denominational

FRIDAY MORNING AND AFTERNOON

WISE the makers of the program, who, after two such strenuous days of great mass meetings, broke the Convention into groups, affording relief from the strain as well as giving the advantage of the closer touch. The State Rallies were held at the various State Headquarters in the nineteen churches set apart for this service, with the exception of Maryland, which took Lyric Hall. At all of these thorough preparations had been made for entertainment of the guests. The church parlors were made most homelike and attractive. Decorations were abundant everywhere, and "Welcome" was written large, not only upon banners but in the greetings. Flowers and banners, palms and pictures, rest-rooms and writing-rooms, newspaper-files and ice-water, — everything that kindly hearts could think of was packed into those rooms to make them delightful and refreshing. And everywhere were the hosts themselves, and the charming hostesses, giving the cordial greetings that came from the heart.

STATE RALLIES

These happy interchanges of courtesies came to a climax in the State Rallies, with their words of greeting and of gratitude. These Rallies, as always, were greatly diversified. Some State delegations, coming from a long distance, were small enough to meet in a church parlor; some taxed to their utmost the largest auditoriums, including the Lyric. Some were informal, some followed elaborate printed programs. Some dealt largely with the business of the State Unions, and others were chiefly inspirational. All were helpful and enjoyable and not least in importance among the week's gatherings. The enthusiasm manifested in these meetings was up to the level of the Armory.

A feature of the Rallies was the wide and hearty endorsement of the Quarter-Century testimonial. In some cases contributions of twenty-five cents per member began to pour in. Illinois, which lays claim to be the first to make a contribution to the project, passed resolutions enthusiastically, as the following shows: —

Whereas, a movement has been inaugurated to commemorate the twenty-fifth anniversary of Christian Endeavor by a suitable memorial building in which to carry on our world-wide work and also to emphasize our love for Dr. Francis E. Clark; therefore,

Resolved, That as representatives of the Christian Endeavor Union of Illinois we most heartily approve this movement and pledge ourselves to sustain it, and would suggest that every Endeavorer in Illinois should contribute at least 25 cents for this purpose at once.

This may be taken as a sample of the resolutions and feeling generally manifested.

The New Jersey Resolution

In addition to the Illinois resolution, this one, passed by the New Jersey Endeavorers enthusiastically, puts the matter in the right way. Mr. Abbott is one of the live leaders and keeps little Jersey to the fore in Endeavor lines.

In view of the unanimous approval, by the Trustees of the United Society, of the suggestion of a headquarters building for the growing needs of the work to provide for a permanent home for the United Society, and to make it thereby self-supporting, and as a lasting memorial to and an appreciation of the self-sacrificing labors of Rev. Francis E. Clark, D. D. (under God the founder of the Christian Endeavor movement), whose valued services have been freely given to the work, without compensation in any way, we, the Endeavorers of the State of New Jersey, assembled in State Rally at the International Convention in Baltimore, do hereby ask our State Executive Committee that they indorse the proposed plan for raising the funds necessary for the erecting of such a building, namely, by the contribution of twenty-five cents from all Christian Endeavorers, Seniors and Juniors, etc., whether members now or formerly, and that they take such steps as in their judgment will secure for every Endeavorer in New Jersey the privilege of being identified with this movement; and to this end we, the delegates assembled, pledge our State officers our most earnest and enthusiastic support and coöperation."

This resolution was heartily concurred in by the Florida delegates present.

Denominational Rallies

Denominational fellowship is heightened by interdenominational fellowship. That is the testimony of thousands who would not for anything give up the blessing that has come from the larger, and who because of the wider circle enjoy the family circle all the more. All talk about denominational disloyalty being bred by interdenominational association like that of Christian Endeavor is the invention of those who are too prejudiced to investigate the facts. The Denominational Rallies have ever been among the most spirited and helpful meetings of the Endeavor Conventions and the same was true this year. They were held in twenty-four of the churches, from three to five o'clock. The attendance was generally large, the addresses were bright and to the point, and the afternoon was full of enjoyment and good fellowship. For the reports which follow, and which are of necessity of the briefest description, we are indebted to the courtesy of the *Christian Endeavor World*, whose Convention Report, by the way, is a masterly piece of condensed descriptive writing and should be in the hands of every Endeavorer.

JOINT PRESBYTERIAN

Place, Lyric Hall, filled. Largest of the Rallies. Led by Rev. John Timothy Brown Stone, of Brown Memorial Church, Baltimore, a bright presiding officer, apt in illustration. Keynote, closer sympathy and coöperation among Presbyterians. Some of the sayings: —

Dr. Allison: Consecrated individuality at home will be felt throughout the world. Let us not only live, let us lift.

Mr. Stone: Nothing is more necessary than world-wide vision. We need to look at the world not simply through our own little lenses, like the girl traveling abroad who complained that the cathedrals were too large for her camera.

B. C. Millikin: I know of no study half so interesting as mission study. We will not pray for what we know nothing about. Motto, "Anywhere, so it be forward."

Rev. Charles Stelzle: Some people think the Presbyterian church an organization affected simply with predestination and conservatism, but they are finding out that it is at the very forefront of some of the most important movements of the day.

Dr. W. J. Darby: A great field stands open in the colleges for Christian Endeavor to impress its ideals upon the young men and women at this formative period.

President Stewart of Auburn: I do so love to think we are coming more and more to look at each other as different branches of the same church, not as U. P.'s, R. P.'s, C. P.'s, or split peas of various kinds. (This made a tremendous hit.)

Prof. J. L. Howe, of University of Virginia: The better we get to know each other, the more we shall find in common. The more isolated a man is, the more he thinks he is unique. The differences between the churches are nothing compared with the identities.

Dr. E. F. Hallenbeck: If we have so much business that we have not time for honest waiting upon God, we have more business than God intended us to have.

This was an exceedingly spirited Rally, and every address was of the best.

THE BAPTISTS

Brantly Church the place, Rev. S. C. Ohrum, of Boston, leader. Theme, "The Love-Feast at St. Louis," where the Baptists of North and South organized a General Convention. Addresses by Rev. Howard B. Grose, New York; Dr. O. P. Gifford, Buffalo; Dr. J. T. Beckley, Boston; Dr. H. A. Griesemer, Baltimore; Rev. E. J. Hewett, Jamaica, W. I., and H. N. Lathrop, Boston.

Mr. Grose described the great meeting in St. Louis, distinguished by the spirit of denominational fellowship, which, he said, when carried into the interdenominational fellowship of Christian Endeavor, is so powerful for the progress of the kingdom of God. Denominational loyalty is not weakened by interdenominational fellowship, but strengthened, just as a true man is stronger when he is broad in spirit and sympathy instead of narrow. United, the Baptists of America will bear their message to the world.

Dr. Gifford: The love-feast at St. Louis means that we have learned Paul's lesson to forget the things that are behind; that we remember Lot's wife, and do not live with our faces one way and our feet another. Lot's wife became a perpendicular pickle because of her folly. St. Louis means that the sons will not carry on the feuds of the fathers. But what of it? The young couple making love in the parlor sit late, for her father pays the gas-bill, and her mother gets the breakfast. Turning from the marriage altar the practical part of life begins. He must pay the bills, and she must get the breakfast. We have had our love-feast; what better will the world be? The new union will mean that the Baptists of America shall do their part in the conquest of the world for Christ.

Dr. Beckley recalled historical incidents connected with Baptist leaders in Baltimore, and predicted an ultimate federation of all baptized believers. Dr. Griesemer believed great good would come from the unity of the Northern and Southern Baptists.

Mr. Hewett, from Jamaica, told of the denominational growth there, until from the start sixty-seven years ago, when the liberation of the slaves took place, there are now one hundred and eighty-eight churches, with more than thirty-three thousand members, and a Baptist college.

Mr. Lathrop predicted closer union, and warned the ministers that if they did not hurry up the laity would take the reins and bring about complete union. The president of the Brantly Memorial Society told of the large work carried on, including support of a missionary abroad and a mission at home.

The Congregationalists

Place, Associate Church, full; leader, Dr. McElveen, of Boston; plenty of enthusiasm and wit; program printed by entertaining church.

Professor Wells explained reasons of Dr. Clark's absence and expounded the proposed Quarter-Century Memorial Building, the project receiving hearty approval.

Greetings from foreign lands by Rev. F. S. Hatch and Dr. Hume, representing India. Secretary Shelton spoke on personal evangelism, and Secretary Hicks gave pointed advice on the concentration of our forces.

Dr. Washington Gladden was received with the honor due to his splendid character and ability, and to his position as moderator of the National Council. Speaking impromptu and most happily, he advised his hearers to "Keep cool," "Keep dry," "Don't dry up," "Get on the right side," and "Keep a-going." President King and Miss Ellen M. Stone were introduced, and spoke brightly.

The most important action was the formation of the Congregational Christian Endeavor Union. The object of this new organization is to unite all young people's societies of religious aims and purposes, connected with Congregational churches, for the advance of the work as a denomination, and for coöperation with the missionary boards and other denominational agencies in the work committed to them.

A full set of officers was elected. President, Dr. McElveen, of Boston; vice-presidents, Dr. Jefferson, of New York, Dr. Mills, of St. Louis, Dr. Adams, of San Francisco, and Dr. Frank G. Smith, of Chicago. Twenty-eight councillors were chosen, — eminent men, representing most of the country from the Atlantic to the Pacific.

The plan of the organization is very simple. It will foster Christian Endeavor among Congregational churches, and hold its biennial meetings in connection with the International Christian Endeavor Conventions.

The Lutherans

Largest ever held; presided over by president National Lutheran Christian Endeavor Union, Rev. P. A. Heilman, of Baltimore. Theme, "The Young People and Missions," and all the addresses had a missionary bearing.

Dr. E. Heyl Delk, of Philadelphia, spoke on "Christian Endeavor as a Missionary," showing the power of the young people in carrying the gospel to the heathen.

Rev. C. H. Butler, of Washington, D. C., spoke on "Christian Endeavor and the Reformation." Then followed three-minute addresses from men and women from all parts of the land.

Rev. F. S. Hatch spoke of his visit to the Lutheran mission in Guntur, India, and the wonderful work they have been doing.

The meeting closed with a stirring address from Dr. A. S. Hootman, of Baltimore, secretary Home Mission Board of the Lutheran Church. He spoke of the possibilities of the young people in enlarging the work and starting missions where they are so much needed.

The Reformed Church in America

Rev. Otto L. F. Mohn, of New York, presided and summoned his hearers to "be of good courage." They showed plenty of enthusiasm.

Rev. E. W. Thompson, recently returned from Oklahoma, where he had been superintending the work of home missions connected with the Reformed Church, urged upon us all an obligation to carry the gospel "to all nations."

Rev. G. H. Eggleston, of Jersey City, spoke on "Some Secrets of Success." Representing a "banner" society, he told of the successful career of the society connected with his church. The members should become more and more mindful and careful of their individual responsibility.

Rev. Harris Freer, of East Greenbush, N. Y., spoke of the need in our several committees of more aggressive Christian work. Dr. Charles H. Tyndall, of Mt. Vernon, urged upon us all our duty and privilege to become "resonant" with "the Holy Spirit," "in tune with the infinite."

African Methodist Episcopal and African Methodist Episcopal Zion Joint Rally

Bishops Arnett and Walters presided jointly. Welcome by Dr. D. G. Hill, of Baltimore; response by Dr. R. W. Fickland, of Philadelphia. Bishop Arnett spoke on Christian Endeavor work.

Dr. B. J. Bolding, of Baltimore, formerly editor of *The Varick Endeavorer*, of the African Methodist Episcopal Zion Church, and Dr. E. J. Gregg, of Jacksonville, Fla., general secretary of the Allen Christian Endeavor societies, spoke of the growth and development of Christian Endeavor principles among the societies; five hundred and four Allen Christian Endeavor leagues have been registered with the general secretary within the last twelvemonth.

Dr. A. L. Gaines, of Baltimore, spoke upon the individual responsibility of each Endeavorer to work for the saving of the lost. Other speakers were Dr. P. H. Williams, of York, Penn.; Dr. O. J. W. Scott, of Washington, D. C.; Dr. D. S. Maten, of Fort Worth, Tex. The attendance was large, and there was much enthusiasm; best of all, much of helpfulness and inspirational force was brought to the ministers, delegates, and the audience.

Several delegates from Baptist churches also reported progress, and pledged their loyalty to Christian Endeavor. The testimonial building proposed was heartily endorsed.

The Methodist Protestants

Place, Lafayette Avenue Methodist Protestant Church; packed; largest Rally the denomination ever held. It was organized in Baltimore in 1828. Rev. James H. Straughn, of Virginia, leader. Chairmen Atwood of Baltimore Committee, representing the five Methodist Protestants of that fine body, called to higher and more aggressive work. Dr. Tagg, president of the General Conference, showed the cordial and sympathetic coöperation of Christian Endeavor in the church work.

Much interest centered in this meeting because for several years efforts have been making to bring about union among this body and the United Brethren and the Congregationalists, also the Primitive Methods. Representatives of each of these denominations were present. All the addresses were cordial.

Dr. E. Humphries, Primitive Methodist of Rhode Island: I am deeply interested in the proposed union and have labored for it. The differences are scarcely discernible, the agreements numerous.

Bishop Mills, United Brethren: We agree in so many things I see no reason why we may not come together.

Dr. Hill, representing Congregationalists: Mere oneness is not harmony; hammering on one key of the organ is not harmony, we want several keys going; but we are brethren.

President Lewis, Methodist Protestant: I am not opposed to union when in the providence of God it shall be advisable, but I am opposed to breaking up my own and bringing it to naught without good reason. Loyalty to our own before we unite with another.

Rev. J. Sala Leland, missionary superintendent of the Denominational Union, showed the good work accomplished; four missionaries are kept in the field.

President Hubbell, of Ohio Union, was witty and epigrammatic. He announced determination to send out a field secretary to develop the Endeavor work. "The West needs us, and the genius of Christian Endeavor is that the stronger East shall support such a work and pass on a good thing."

THE DISCIPLES

Place, Harlem Avenue Christian Church; filled. Leader, Rev. E. B. Bagby, of Washington. A roll-call of States brought responses from nearly all, also from England, Mexico, Jamaica, and India. Splendid reports of progress, increase, and good work of many kinds; much enthusiasm. Rev. Mr. Hatch told of the Disciples' missionaries in India, their worthiness and devotion.

The climax was reached at the close, when Rev. B. A. Abbott, pastor of the entertaining church, and a member of the Committee of 1905, gave this ringing exhortation as his advice to the Disciples of Christ: —

"*Let us stand by Christian Endeavor with all our might.* I know of no other movement or agency which has done and is likely to do so much toward realizing one of the objects for which we stand and for which the Master prayed — the unity of His people." This was received with the greatest applause.

UNITED EVANGELICAL CHURCH

This denomination has the Keystone League of Christian Endeavor, showing how the denominational and interdenominational can be combined effectively. There was a large rally at the Olive Branch Church, a new house of worship. Of the four hundred present, forty-four were ministers. Addresses were made by Mr. J. B. Girardin, Rev. L. S. Reichard, Dr. J. F. Dunlap, General Secretary Fouke, of the managing board, President Poling, of Dallas College, and Editor W. M. Stanford, of the *Evangelical*, Harrisburg, Pa.

Dr. Stanford on the Importance of Junior Work: This appears, 1. From Bible authority and emphasis placed upon it; 2. In saving the children for their own sake; 3. In rendering effective service to the church; 4. In the length of service it secures; 5. In the rich reward for service among the Juniors.

A pleasant feature was the introduction by the leader of the ministers present from the Atlantic to the Pacific coast. After they were all standing before the audience they were asked to sing; and a fine, impressive, spiritual song service ensued.

Motto: Always and all for Jesus.

THE UNITED BRETHREN

In charge of Dr. H. F. Shupe. Special emphasis on church union, the subject presented happily and earnestly by Rev. Charles H. Hubbell, Methodist Protestant; Dr. Hill, Congregationalist; Bishop Mills, of United Brethren Church; but so far as Christian Endeavorers are concerned, there was no need of argument in favor of the union of these churches.

Mr. Claude H. Eckert, of Akron, O., spoke on "Christian Endeavor for the United Brethren Church." Porto Rico was represented by Miss Elizabeth Reed, a teacher of Ponce; Africa, by Mrs. Mary E. Albert, who told of the three hundred

United Brethren Endeavorers in Sierra Leone, West Africa; and Japan, by Rev. J. Edgar Knipp, who described our young men's Christian Endeavor Society in Kyoto.

The Endeavorers of the Salem Church, where the rally was held, served supper to the two hundred and fifty people present.

REFORMED CHURCH IN THE UNITED STATES

Dr. Rufus G. Miller, leader. Missions was the dominant thought. Dr. A. R. Bartholomew, president Pennsylvania Union, and secretary of the Board of Foreign Missions, told of the action of the General Synod asking the Young People's societies to support two missionaries in Japan and China. One is already in the field, and five hundred dollars is pledged toward the second.

F. G. Hobson, Esq., member of the Board of Home Missions, pleaded for a Christian Endeavor home missionary. Dr. Rufus W. Miller represented the denominational reading-course and mission-study classes. Delegates from Tiffin, O., Philadelphia, Reading, Washington, D. C., Hagerstown, Md., etc., testified of the missionary work of their societies.

Mr. Shartle, of Reading, roused great enthusiasm by the story of the Christain Endeavor Society of Virginsville, Penn., out of which a congregation was organized and a church built.

"Everybody at work" was the summing up of Dr. C. Clews, Hagerstown, Md.

Attendance large and representative, Indiana, Ohio, Pennsylvania, Maryland, and other States being represented.

THE EPISCOPALIANS

Dr. Floyd W. Tomkins in charge. He spoke on the meaning of the Convention and of the Christian Endeavor Society, the need of the Episcopal Church for the Society, and the Society's adaptability. He mentioned the deepening of the spiritual life and the holding of the young people as two inevitable results: also the effect upon the minister's new spiritual life when he took a lively interest in the Society.

Rev. E. H. Dickerson, assistant at St. Peter's Church, where the rally was held, gave hearty welcome, and urged the work as most worthy of adoption by every Episcopal Church.

Mr. W. A. Schumacher, chairman of the Convention reception committee, and an active member of St. Peter's, made a ringing speech telling of his experiences at the Convention and elsewhere.

Rev. C. J. Palmer, of Lanesboro, Mass., gave the leading address. Mr. Palmer was in Portland, and knew many of the members of the first Christian Endeavor Society when Dr. Clark started it. He has done much Christian Endeavor work, has written much literature, and has corresponded largely in the interest of Christian Endeavor. He emphasized the pledge, lookout work, and consecration meeting as the three marked characteristics making Christian Endeavor a power. He urged a variety in the meetings, and made many helpful suggestions, such as a monthly praise service, regular and exact missionary meetings, and meetings for communion.

Rev. Mr. Hensel, of Baltimore, also spoke, and a few others. The meeting was profitable, and will result in good.

THE METHODISTS

The three branches of Methodism — the Methodist Episcopal, Methodist Episcopal South, and Canadian Methodists — clasped hands and sang together, "Blest be the tie that binds our hearts in Christian love."

Dr. George J. Burns, who presided, spoke of "The Progressive Spirit of Methodism," how the Methodist Episcopal Church was organized at the Christmas

Conference held in Lovely Lane Chapel, Baltimore, in 1784. There were then eighty-three preachers occupying circuits and stations. Now Methodism is a world-power.

Rev. J. F. Heisse: We are upon historic ground. This place was made famous by men of God, such as the orator, Thomas Guard, and the soul-winner, J. O. Peck. This is a city of Methodism. We have not lost the class-meeting, the love-feast, or the altar service; hundreds of souls are being converted every year.

President John F. Goucher: There are three essentials, catholicity, loyalty to the denomination, and personality. The need of the times is broad men sharpened to a point, men who can reach out and by faith grasp the earth and at the same time the throne of God.

Bishop Alpheus W. Wilson: It would be a hard thing to go anywhere in this country where you would not find a Methodist. Methodism goes for everybody. Christian Endeavor indicates that you have a type of work to do that no one else can perform. Our work is whatever Christ would have us do. Men waste their time and strength when they undertake any other work.

In the "Open Parliament" two subjects were considered: "The Model Methodist" and "The Model Christian Endeavorer."

The United and Reformed Presbyterians

Another joint rally, encouraging, helpful, and inspiring. The devotional exercises were conducted by Dr. T. C. Atchison, pastor of North Avenue United Presbyterian Church, where the rally was held, Dr. J. B. Wilson, First United Presbyterian Church, Baltimore, welcomed the delegates.

Dr. W. H. McMillan, Allgeheny, Penn., declared: "I believe with all my soul that every young people's society in the United Presbyterian Church should be a Christian Endeavor society." "A strong pledge makes a strong society. The pledge is the spinal column of the young people's movement." "When Christian Endeavorers come to be old, they will not be the mossbacks in the church of Jesus Christ."

"Loyalty to Christ" was the theme of Dr. R. C. Wylie, of Wilkensberg, Penn. Rev. Mr. Blair, of Utica, O., spoke on the usefulness of Christian Endeavor to the church.

Dr. Samuel McNaugher, of Boston, spoke on "The Use of Psalms in Religious Worship." A social hour, with refreshments, followed.

The Brethren

Deep earnestness and an intense love for the cause characterized the best Rally ever held by the Brethren at an International Convention.

Rev. C. F. Yoder, trustee of the United Society, spoke on "The Mission of the Christian Endeavor Movement." It has trained the young people in cooperation, consecration, practical service, good citizenship, mission work, giving, and in personal work.

"The Place of the Brethren among the Denominations," was treated by Rev. L. S. Bauman, of the Grace Church, Philadelphia.

A brief address was made by Rev. J. S. Bowers, pastor of the Clark Memorial Independent Methodist Church, in which the Rally was held.

Rev. Zed H. Copp, of Washington, D. C., spoke on "Building a Christian Endeavor Boom." His earnest appeal was couched in six "p's"; perception, push, power, patience, persistence, and purse.

"A Forward Look," by the leader, Rev. George C. Carpenter, of Warsaw, Ind. We need to aim at greater efficiency in our societies, as well as greater numbers. We need a traveling secretary; but, as that is impossible at present, every pastor ought to be a first-class assistant to the general secretary. Do you want our church to grow? Then push Christian Endeavor. Do you want more workers? Then push Christian Endeavor. Do you want more efficient workers?

Then push along Christian Endeavor. Yes, Mr. Shaw, we like to see Christian Endeavor "die the way it is dying. We like to see it wane the way it is waning."

THE REFORMED EPISCOPALIANS

Bishop Samuel Fallows, of Chicago, presided at the enthusiastic gathering, and made the opening address. He said: The Christian Endeavor movement has gloriously enlarged the idea of Reformed Episcopalianism, which means loyalty to evangelical Christianity and the recognition of the holy catholic church, which is the communion of saints. Therefore the Reformed Episcopal Church must ever be the stanch defender of Christian Endeavorism. In every parish Christian Endeavor societies should be formed and developed, if not already organized.

Rev. H. Medley Price, rector of the Bishop Cummins Memorial Church, where the Rally was held, said: This International Convention of Christian Endeavor is the greatest religious event which ever occurred in Baltimore. We can have church unity only by coming together as in Christian Endeavor, members of one family, with the specific individuality of each one fully preserved.

Rev. Dr. May, rector of the Church of the Reconciliation, Baltimore, said: The things that have impressed me most in the Convention are the grand demonstrations of Christian unity, the mighty power of religious enthusiasm, and the magnificent music and singing.

Rev. Duane Wevill, rector of the Church of the Redeemer, Baltimore, said: The Christian Endeavor movement determined me to become a minister of Christ. One of my Christian Endeavor boys has become one of the ministers in a most important church in Chicago.

Mr. Richard A. Harris, one of the musical directors of the Convention, said: I have been led to a richer and fuller Christian life through my connection with the great Endeavor host. I meet the grandest men and women in the church at large through my relationship to it.

Other remarks were made by different speakers, and resolutions of greeting and sympathy were sent to the Reformed Episcopal Endeavorers in India.

Seldom are finer testimonials given to the influence of Christian Endeavor.

THE FRIENDS

The following program was given: —

J. Edgar Williams, of Greensboro, N. C., spoke on "The Ministry and Christian Endeavor," emphasizing especially the value of Christian Endeavor in developing the gifts of young people in the ministry.

Lewis E. Stout, of Plainfield, Ind., spoke on "Ebenezer; thus far hath the Lord helped us." The stones, memorial of God's help to us in Christian Endeavor thus far, he named: For Christ and the Church, humility, individuality, and coöperation.

Elbert Russell, of Earlham College, Richmond, Ind., presided, and spoke on the features of Christian Endeavor work and organization which have been characteristic of Friends, such as individual initiative in worship, silent worship, equality of women with men in worship, peace, a non-military ideal of citizenship, and congregational polity.

The Rally concluded in a social, at which the local church served refreshments.

THE CHURCH OF GOD

Well-attended Rally, addressed by Rev. A. E. Kepford, State president of Iowa; Rev. C. H. Grove, of Roaring Spring, Penn.; Rev. J. M. Waggoner, of Altoona, Penn.; Rev. George Hulm, of Latrobe, Penn.; President C. I. Brown, of Findlay, O.; and others. The subjects that received most attention were evangelism, missions, and education.

Dr. C. I. Brown was in charge.

The Free Baptists

The delegates represented Nova Scotia and five of the States. Mr. Harry S. Myers, of Hillsdale, Mich., general secretary of the United Society of Free Baptist Young People, had charge. The Rally was an informal conference, in which all present compared notes and made suggestions in enlarging the number of societies, increasing the membership, and securing more work. Mission-study, Junior societies, and evangelism were the topics discussed.

The Moravians

Distinct, enthusiastic emphasis was laid by the Rally upon personal work, mission-study classes, and evangelistic activity.
Rev. William H. Vogler was the leader.

MT. ROYAL STATION OF THE BALTIMORE & OHIO R.R.

SEA LION POND, DRUID HILL PARK, BALTIMORE

CHAPTER X

Evangelism

AT THE ARMORY, FRIDAY EVENING

AFTER the day's separation, the hosts came together again at night in the Armory and Lyric Hall. There had been a downpour of rain in the morning, which interfered somewhat with the State Rallies, and which drenched thousands of Endeavorers, whose umbrellas proved little protection against such driving sheets of water. It was a weather week without doubt. Yet after all this and a hot and humid afternoon, the crowds came up smiling for another great evening of inspiration.

The subject at the Armory was Evangelism, and this was rightly said, by Dr. F. D. Power, of Washington, who presided, to be the subject of all subjects. Fortunately for the Christian Church it is quite the uppermost subject at the present time among nearly all of the evangelical denominations.

Before the session the Minneapolis delegation marched about the hall, distributing tiny bags of flour and giving their yell, in an effort to boom their beautiful city for the next convention. This brought other places to the front also, and there was a good deal of enthusiasm engendered.

The song service was led by Mr. Foster, and the devotional service was conducted by Dr. Darby, of Indiana, one of the efficient Trustees. The rendering of Gounod's anthem, "Gentle, Holy Saviour," was so exquisite that an encore was demanded. Dr. Power read the following telegrams, which explain themselves: —

DR. FRANCIS E. CLARK, *Pine Point, Me.*

Minnesota, which hopes to be the place of the meeting of the next Convention, sends a message of greeting, with love and sympathy.

(Signed) ANNA L. SMITH,
Secretary State Union.

A box of roses was also sent by Minnesota.

DR. FRANCIS E. CLARK, *Pine Point, Me.*

The Maine Endeavorers at Baltimore send love and pray for your speedy and complete recovery.

(Signed) CHARLES D. CRANE,
Field Secretary Maine C. E. U.

SANTA BARBARA, CAL.

INTERNATIONAL CHRISTIAN ENDEAVOR CONVENTION:

Following our most spiritual State Convention, greetings. Isaiah, xli. 6.

1905 COMMITTEE,
State Convention now in Session.

TO THE WORLD'S CONVENTION OF CHRISTIAN ENDEAVORERS AT BALTIMORE:

The Christian Endeavor Union of Southport, England, sends greeting: "We cease not to give thanks for you, making mention of you in our prayers, that the God of our Lord Jesus Christ, the Father of Glory, may give unto you the spirit of wisdom and revelation in the knowledge of Him."

KANSAS CITY, MO.

MR. GUY M. WITHERS, BALTIMORE:

Directors of Young Men's Christian Association heartily indorse Kansas City for the Christian Endeavor Convention, 1907.

(Signed) CARL S. BISHOP,
General Secretary, Kansas City Y. M. C. A.

In introducing the first speaker, Dr. Power told how Christian Endeavorers might save the world in five years by repeating a simple process of doubling, each one winning one more to Christ. Then he made the appeal, "Shall we all go home from this Convention determined to win at least one soul to Christ this year?"

Dr. O. P. Gifford, of Buffalo, whose theme was "Evangelism Abroad," was at his best. Always keen, epigrammatic, with sentences clear as his thought, and aptly illustrative, he made a deep impression. Rain was not falling, for a wonder, and the speakers could make themselves fairly well heard by the great congregation, which was an amazement after such trying experiences. Dr. Gifford said in part: —

Christ came to a hopeless, heartbroken race. "Ah," you tell me, "but that was eighteen hundred years ago, and there is evolution." Evolution! Is the heathen world any nearer God to-night than it was when Paul trod the streets of Ephesus? Is it not without hope and without God? Is it not alien to the commonwealth of truth? It would take longer than God's eternity to evolve a heathen nation into a saved people. When Dr. Ashmore, our prime minister of missionaries, went to China, he translated Paul's epistle to the Romans. He handed it out, and they read it, and sneered, and said: "You wrote it since you came. It is a picture of our civilization." The world needs the gospel of the Son of God as much as it needed it when the first missionaries started.

The genius of the Christian religion is missionary. Christ bade His followers go into all the world and preach the gospel. But does the world need the gospel? So long as Christians cannot stand on the temple area in Jerusalem without a guard, men need the gospel. Need a message that will break down walls of partition, and through the rent veil bring all men side by side, face to face, with God. Need a religion that will reveal God to all alike, and enable men to live without fighting.

There is nothing more pitiable in all the earth than a godless man. A derelict on the sea of time, without compass or port, simply adrift; a blind man in a world flooded with light; a deaf man in a universe throbbing with music; an idiot in a library; a dead man adrift upon a sea of life. Ah, sirs, it is bad enough to be friendless, but to be godless, I would rather not be. Vastly better to blot me out than to leave me and blot God out, for without Him life is a burden and a curse.

A Toronto paper of a late date had a map of Manchuria, with the Russian troops deployed as black blocks, and Oyama, standing with outstretched arms, reaching around to gather the mail in. This is the gospel, the Son of Man reaching around the nations of the earth to gather them all into his new kingdom. No one doubts Japan's desire to reach around and capture Russia's army. Do you doubt Christ's desire to conquer the world? Do you believe that Christ stands with outstretched arm seeking to embrace a redeemed humanity? If so, it becomes your duty and mine to proclaim our faith, nay more, to be muscular fiber in the outstretched arms to surround and gather the world to the heart of Christ.

On May 23 the *Christian Endeavor World* published the program of this Convention. As I opened the copy, I saw on the opposite page a statement that the government had been at work in the great West, and had learned that under the Great American Desert, given over to death, were great lakes and rivers, and all that men needed to do was to drive an artesian well a hundred feet, and the water would gush up, and the desert would blossom as the rose. It is for you and me to go to the world in its desert struggles and teach it how to reach the gospel of Christ.

It is the will of Christ that the world be evangelized; it is the need of the world that it be evangelized; it is the duty of the Christian Endeavor Society to evangelize the world according to the will of Jesus Christ.

While the audience was singing "Christ for the world" at the close of Dr. Gifford's address, Dr. Gladden came over from the Lyric, where he had spoken, and was introduced, but said simply, "I have nothing to say but just that old song the heathen man learned to sing — the only two words he knew of the English language, and he made them into a song,

"'Go on, go on, go on, go on,
Go on, go on, go on, go on,
Go on, go on, go on, go on,
Go on, go on, go on, go on.'

You can sing it if you want to."

He was greeted with a warmth that evinced the hold his high moral and ethical teaching has upon the young people.

The second and closing address was by Dr. Mark Allison Matthews, of Seattle. He was one of the most striking figures that has appeared on the Endeavor platform, and that is saying a good deal. Six feet four or more in height, spare to a degree, with a head of hair as remarkable as height and figure, he would be noted anywhere. Soon he proved himself to be an incisive and epigrammatic speaker, brilliant and sparkling, and apt to make the most of a point. Such speakers must be allowed some license, and if he seemed to bear down pretty hard upon the faults of others, as he saw them, his aim was doubtless that of the reformer. Here are some of his crisp sentences: —

The saddest day America has recorded in her calendar is that day in the past when she placed her family Bible and her hymn-book upon the center-table, there to molder beneath the rust of social entertainment. The church, to reach her former position of power, must reach it by way of the family altar and God's Word accompanied by family singing.

The individual doing personal work, seeking out and bringing to Christ the lost man, is ideal Christianity. Every man should make his disciple. The greatest need of the pulpit to-day is an imperishable passion for souls. No minister should be allowed to go into his pulpit who has not planned for, prepared for, prayed for, and who does not expect, conversions as immediate results of his preaching.

Given a Spirit-filled, praying pastor, preaching the great doctrines of the gospel of blood, followed by a consecrated force with a passion for souls, and you will have an open, live, and influential church, to which the Holy Spirit will add daily such as are saved at every service. The trouble with us is, we play at the business of preaching and leading men to Christ. Let us cease playing, and become active, zealous, consecrated workers, and God will give us the world for Christ.

The problem is the Christianization of America. The remedy is pastoral evangelism. The pastor is responsible for the condition in his local field. He is the leader; therefore, if he is lazy and spiritless and indifferent his church will in a short time become a congregation of sleeping saints. When pastors are afflicted with indefiniteness it is impossible for a church to succeed. This country must be saved and saved quick. The problem is gigantic. Pagan influences are at work and their power is now being felt. Commercialism is insane and money-making is a universal disease. Dishonesty in low and high places is arrogant and unblushing. Political corruption is entrenched. We have become accustomed to and contented with wickedness. To be accustomed to wickedness is an awful state.

In the future every man who exercises the principle of municipal suffrage shall be known as a decent citizen or a damnable grafter. Capital and labor shall be made to recognize the Golden Rule and live by its teachings. The church shall be revived and sent on its evangelistic mission. The remedy is pastoral evangelism. There are three kinds of evangelism — professional, personal, pastoral. Pastoral is the God-honored kind. Drawing the net after every service is the pastor's plain duty. Turn every occasion into an opportunity to preach a risen and living Christ. Recognize that the church is the pastor's force and not his field. It is not his business to spend his days listening to female whiners and masculine croakers. It is his duty to organize his force, master the geography of his field, and lead his army to victory. To organize, work, and lead a church is a profession. True pastoral evangelism is Christianity set on fire. The church ought to be a missionary society in the field; ought to be in a state of revival all the time.

The audience felt the force of the gripping sentences, delivered with personal power, and frequently applauded the good points. The whole service gave impetus to the evangelistic impulse. There was regret at the absence of Dr. Hillis, whose physician bade him take a rest instead of keeping his engagement in Baltimore, but no disappointments of any kind, not even the supreme one of Dr. Clark's illness, could check the splendid spirit of this great Convention, one of the most earnest in all our history.

In closing the service Dr. Power remarked that more than two million brought to Christ by Christian Endeavorers showed that the Society is an evangelistic agency, and urged that such work be made more and more the business of Christian Endeavor.

CHAPTER XI

Christian Culture for Christian Service

AT LYRIC HALL

THIS was the second evening of dual sessions, and again the charming Lyric Hall was filled with listeners, many of them drawn by the name of Washington Gladden, who was to speak on "The Education of Conscience," a most important subject to be treated by a man whose life has largely been devoted to the study of ethics and social problems. Dr. Gladden had to make a train, and everything had to bend to that. The song service was under direction of Mr. Jacobs, who brought the best spirit out of the audience in the few moments in which he had them singing. Prof. J. L. Howe, of Washington and Lee University, an esteemed Southern Trustee, was in charge. After prayer by Bishop Walters, he introduced, "without any titles, for he does not need them, Washington Gladden, the moderator of the Congregational National Council." Dr. Gladden read from manuscript, and lost much of impression from this circumstance. What he said was more weighty than the manner of his saying it, but the hearers appreciated his sharp analysis of motive and his plea for rigid obedience to an enlightened conscience.. The entire address would make most profitable reading, but only an abstract can be given:—

There is a tremendous amount of uneducated or miseducated conscience in this country to-day. People in good society — people who are members of our churches — people who are known as our leading citizens, are doing things which are horribly wrong, and neither do their own consciences protest, nor is there any moral sense in the community which adequately disapproves their wrongdoing. The things which have been going on of late can only be explained upon the theory of a general slump of conscience in financial circles and in political circles, in society and, most deplorable of all, in the church itself.

The one thing this country needs most to-day is not better laws, nor better methods of administration, but a clearing up and toning up of the consciences of its citizens.

There is great need of sharpening the conscience with respect to the principles of common honesty. The phenomenon known as "graft" is a widespread and deadly disregard of the primary rights of property. The essence of it is the appropriation for personal uses of public or private property held in trust.

A simple instance of this, he said, was the appropriation of official stationery for other than official purposes by a Congressman or a member of a State Legislature. Another "grafter," he said, is the public official who takes a journey for his own pleasure at the public charge. As other types of public "grafters" he cited the man who tries to hide his property from the eyes of the tax assessor, so that he may escape a fair share of taxation, and also the official who uses his office to inaugurate a public improvement because it will benefit his own property, but which the public does not really need.

"If one could believe all that he hears," he continued, "and could accept the estimates of active business men who ought to know whereof they speak, one would be compelled to believe that not only the public service, but private business, is honeycombed with bribery of this sort — that the majority of those who are acting in a functionary capacity as the agents of others are taking their own 'rake-offs' whenever they can do it without detection. I am inclined to think that these estimates are largely exaggerated so far as private business is concerned, but my knowledge of public business constrains me to believe that the evil prevails in that to an appalling extent.

"The trouble is that the consciences of men have become fearfully dulled and perverted in all these matters. They have come to look with tolerance and indifference upon them. That is true, I fear, of most of us. If we do not exactly approve, we do not feel that it matters very much. It is nothing to make a fuss about. The people who do such things lose no caste; they move in the best society; we elect them superintendents of our Sunday-schools and deacons and elders in our churches.

"If our consciences were properly educated we should see very clearly that all these things are nothing but theft. There is not a particle of difference in God's sight between the man who takes his 'rake-off' on a public contract and the man who picks your pocket; between a man who goes on a junket at the public expense and the man who raises a check and appropriates money. It is simple stealing — nothing else. It is not a bit more respectable than the operations of the sneak thief or green-goods man. And if the Christian conscience had anything like the vigor and clearness it ought to possess it would make these things so infamous that the man who perpetrated them could not stay in the community.

"The greatest injustices of the present day are those that are so widely diffused and so finely divided that their enormity escapes notice. Most of the great fortunes of the day have been built up from a multitude of small extortions, vast in the aggregate, but individually unperceived. There never was so much need of an intelligent and heroic purpose to discover and condemn injustice as there is to-day."

Another truth that should be emphasized, Dr. Gladden said, was the individual responsibility for corporate action. Corporations have almost unlimited power to inflict injustice and suffering, and wherever there is injustice and suffering somebody is to blame for it. Ordinarily, he said, the stockholders will shelter themselves behind the corporation; but what is everybody's business is nobody's business and the injustice goes on.

"If a corporation has no conscience," Dr. Gladden said, "every officer of the corporation has, and it is his business to see to it that nothing is done that his individual conscience could not sanction. The officers are directly responsible for the management of the affairs. If these are conducted in such a way that an officer's conscience cannot approve of them, then let him get out of it and stay not on the order of his going."

But the stockholders share the responsibility with the directors of any concern, he said.

"If a man's money is invested in a company," he continued, "and he is drawing profits out of it, he ought to be satisfied that its business is honest and beneficent. If it is not and cannot be reformed he ought to dispose of his stock and refuse to profit by its iniquity."

His parting word was: "If you want your conscience to be enlightened, obey it. You won't make much progress if you are constantly trampling it down or arguing it down with cries of expediency. Remember, it is the voice by which God speaks to you."

After Mr. Jacobs had sung one of his most impressive solos and been obliged to respond to an encore, a second address was made, on

"The Need for Christian Schools," by President T. H. Lewis, of Western Maryland College. It was a scholarly, finely thoughtful address, one of the best of the Convention, and its significance grew more and more upon the audience, until his points were frequently and warmly applauded. He said in part: —

There can be no Christian culture without Christian schools. What we do not put into the school we cannot get out of the culture.

What is a Christian school? If we define a school as an institution for the promotion of culture, and if we accept Matthew Arnold's definition of culture as the learning and promulgating of the best that is known and thought in the world, we do not narrow the definition by prefixing Christian to it. For we do not mean to restrict this learning and promulgating to Christianity as a theological system, much less to the divergences in Christian teaching represented by denominationalism.

A Christian school is everything that any other school can be, and it is more. This "plus" that differentiates it is not only its reason for existing. It is this which makes it the salt of the intellectual world.

Let me crave your special attention to my description of this plus, for all I have to say evolves from it. A Christian school is an institution where the best that is thought and known in the world is learned and promulgated under the illumination of Christian ideas and the inspiration of the Christian spirit.

What are Christian ideas? Although far-reaching and tremendous in their import, the distinctively Christian ideas are few. The constructive genius of sympathetic Christianity has compressed them into one sentence, "to wit, that God was in Christ reconciling the world unto himself." This is Christianity's creed and program. Here we have defined its source, God; its exponent, Christ; its purpose, reconciliation, and its sphere, the world. Considered as a body of religious doctrine, this outlines for us a theology, a Christology, an anthropology and a sociology. But, taken in a wider sense, as leading and dominating ideas of universal knowledge, this gives us a Christian science, a Christian philosophy, a Christian ethics, and a Christian politics — the perfect square of truth, the best that can be known and thought in the world.

I would insist upon teaching these four great aspects of truth under the illumination of Christian ideas, not to get Christianity taught, but to get these subjects fully taught; that, instead of giving our children partial and distorted glimpses of the truth, we might reveal to them "the depth of the riches both of the wisdom and knowledge of God."

The Christian asks of the scientist only that he pursue his method rigorously where it leads him; physically as far as he can, intellectually when the physical fails, and then to go on where the intellectual inevitably leads him to follow his highest faculty of faith.

How much lower must we fall before we can be persuaded that the world of law and government and business must be a chaos until the light of Christian ideas broods over it? What will convince us that no nation can flourish on universal rottenness? How long will Christian churches continue to pray, "God save the commonwealth?" and leave the schools free to train up citizens on the theory that God has no rightful place in the commonwealth?

It is the teachers that make a school great, not equipment. It is the Christian man in the professor's chair that makes a school Christian. The Christian spirit will have the right of way in our schools if the people are loyal to it.

The members of the chorus, nearly four hundred strong, rendered an anthem beautifully, and then came the closing feature of the evening — a musical object lesson, by Prof. Howard B. Grose. "Music in the Society" was the program title. The speaker got his audience by assuring them there was one point upon which there would be perfect agreement, however much they might differ about music — namely, that it was awfully hot. They laughed and listened, and briskly and attractively he plunged into the subject with a deserved compliment to Baltimore's splendid chorus, this bringing applause from all sides. He said the kind of music heard in the Convention exactly illustrated his thought of what religious music should be — devotional, emotional, educational, and inspirational; a means of spiritual grace and culture. Music plays an important part in the religious life. To show how devotionally a meeting may be opened he had the choir sing a verse of "Day is dying in the West." Music has often been called the handmaid of religion, he said, but to be that it must not be machine-made music, nor concert hall ragtime. Music in the society should be bright and pleasing; good music need not be dull or lifeless, but it should induce the spirit of worship, reverence, prayer and praise, and this could not be done by the ditty, dance, or jig style of stuff that was so common, put out to make money. He told of an experience at a meeting where he was to speak on Sunday-school music, and prepared a caricature, using Yankee Doodle as tune; when lo, the first book he had handed to him at the meeting had in it a tune for kindergartners which was the baldest kind of plagiarism of Yankee Doodle; and presently he came on "Here's to good old Yale, drink her down," used without any credit, and for those beautiful words, "Have you had a kindess shown, pass it on." He had another of the exquisite hymns in the Endeavor Hymnal sung, to show what real music is, and then said, "Let us strive to elevate the musical standards in our societies. We want neither mush, gush, slush, nor rush pieces, but noble sentiment wedded to elevating and touching music." Another example of the genuine hymn that moves the soul to nobler issues, and the brisk and unusual exercise came to an end. The audience, and especially the choir, greatly enjoyed the object lesson, and applause was abundant at every spicy point made on the waltz tunes and trashy words that are flooding the market and degrading the children and young people wherever these cheap books are used.

At the close of this strong session the ever-active California Endeavorers, bent on securing the next Convention for Los Angeles, threw upon the screen a large number of most alluring California views.

MT. VERNON PLACE, IN THE HEART OF THE CONVENTION CITY

CHAPTER XII

An Earned Play Day

A DAY off for excursions, or rest, or what not, after steady going to meeting. That was another wise provision. Tired nature must be consulted, especially during such a week. There was plenty going on, however. Two special features attracted the thousands — one an excursion to Washington, with a gathering on the Capitol steps and addresses of patriotic character by Bishop Fallows, of Chicago, and Commissioner Macfarland, of the District of Columbia; the second an excursion to the battle field of Gettysburg, where an address was to be given by Dr. Hill, of Salem. For those who stayed in Baltimore there was a city worth seeing, including the burnt district now rapidly being rebuilt, and handsomely too; and for several hundred invited guests, including officers and speakers, as guests of the Baltimore Committee, a ride down the bay on a steamer in the afternoon.

To speak of the last first, it may be said that this trip afforded the leaders the first really invigorating and fresh air of the week, and was a boon indeed. If only the ride could have continued until old ocean was reached, and a session or two have been held on board. Yet the invigoration had been received, and all were grateful. It was a delightful social occasion, giving opportunity for acquaintance not otherwise possible. A pleasing incident of the voyage was the playing of "The Star Spangled Banner" by the band on board just as the boat passed Fort McHenry, whose flying flag inspired Key to write the famous tune that will live as long as the nation does that flies the stars and stripes.

AT WASHINGTON

Four or five thousand Endeavorers took advantage of the excursion to the Capital, and were heartily welcomed. A large number went to Mt. Vernon, about the only place on the continent Washington would recognize could he return in person to see the country he once ruled. Sightseers began to leave Baltimore as early as six in the morning, and Washington was given over to them from early morning till late evening. Reception committees were at the stations, and everything was done to make the day enjoyable.

The Rally took place at 3.30 on the East Capitol steps, where the inauguration ceremonies are held. More than two thousand participated in this service, at which Director Percy S. Foster led the singing, as he did in 1896, and Bishop Fallows was in charge of the program. The prayer was offered by former Chaplain Butler of the House, and of course "My country, 'tis of thee," was sung first of all. Commissioner Macfarland made an eloquent speech, in the course of which he said: —

> In yourselves and as representatives of the millions of Christian Endeavorers throughout the world you are very welcome to the capital of the United States — the national capital of most of you. It still remembers gratefully the meeting of your International Convention here in 1896, and is glad to share with its friendly neighbor, Baltimore, in the entertainment of the International Convention of 1905. All Americans worthy of the name want to come to Washington. It is a patriotic pleasure. And Washington wants them all to come, and all the world, besides. Representing the republic in its growth and development faithfully and at all times, it stands now for the power and beauty and majesty to which our country has come. The summed-up history from Christopher Columbus through George Washington to Theodore Roosevelt appears in this sacred place, the east front of the Capitol, where you are now assembled. You see where all the presidents, except George Washington and John Adams, have taken from the chief justice of the United States the oath of office. The very air is filled with memories of great men, great speeches, great decisions, great debates, great acts of government. Here war has been declared and peace made, the great Book of Statutes has been written, and the Constitution and the laws have been interpreted.
> From the dishonesty of high financiers, from the corruption of low politicians, from the immorality of individuals, from the money-madness of many and the pleasure-madness of more, from selfishness in all its forms, every one a disobedience to the heavenly vision, we turn to the millions who fear God and love their country and who would rather be right than rich, faithful than famous, who are doing their duty as patriots in peace, just as they would do their duty as patriots in war, and who thereby are saving their country daily by noble and heroic living. Because we believe that you represent just such people, the great body of our fellow-citizens, we rejoice as we look forward from this high place to-day to the years that are to come out of the East, and in which you young people will gradually take over the responsibilities of carrying on the affairs, of maintaining the honor, and advancing the glory of our dear country.

Bishop Fallows spoke briefly, paying high tributes to President Roosevelt and the late Secretary Hay. Then the company rose and sang "The Star Spangled Banner," everybody waving flags, handkerchiefs, or fans. It was a pretty sight, reminding one of the Washington Convention.

At Gettysburg

A celebration 142 miles long, continuous performance, was the way Dr. Hill described the excursion to Gettysburg, which drew more than twelve hundred of the Convention delegates.

Assembled on the field where the greatest battle and what is conceded to be the decisive conflict of the Civil War was fought, were residents of North and South — from Maine to the Gulf of Mexico and from the Atlantic to the Pacific. The feelings of the past were forgotten in the significant questions of the present. Descendants of one-time bitter opponents clasped hands in concord with universal feelings, and with only brotherly love and fellowship in their hearts they stood side by side under the protecting and glorious banner of the Christian Endeavor.

The delegates were taken to Gettysburg over the Western Maryland Railroad in two special trains. Every State represented at the Convention had some of its delegates on the train. Reaching Gettysburg at 12.30 o'clock, the delegates immediately took carriages and proceeded to East Cemetery Hill, on the Federal lines, where Dr. Hill addressed them. The carriages lined up, and Dr. Hill, after securing an advantageous position, talked to them while they remained in their seats in the conveyances. He is at his best on such occasions, and the eloquent address taught the lessons of the battle and the war. A single passage is all we can give here: —

> It is especially appropriate that you should visit this field, for you could almost say that the battle was fought on the Union side by boys. The average age of the participants in the Battle of Gettysburg was twenty-three years. When you see soldiers dedicating monuments, decorating graves, attending memorial services, you will have to think that it was by no such gray, grizzled, aged persons that our most radiant and conspicuous and far-reaching and overwhelming victory was achieved. The boys did it. The typical American soldier seems to have been a youth. His valor, heroism, devotion, and spirit saved us our united land.
>
> It is a striking feature of Gettysburg that it supplies precisely the element that, for example, Chancellorsville lacks. In the latter battle the soldiers were not defeated. The generals were outclassed, and simply and ridiculously whipped. Our great defeat and humiliation arose from the fact that there were 37,000 young, brave men that our generals did not seem to be able to introduce into the fight. This is a lesson for pastors and Christian workers and leaders. Here were troops eager for the fray, but they lacked direction. Vicksburg stands as a great achievement of a general. When Grant dropped down the Mississippi River, cut himself loose from the base of supplies and informed the authorities at Washington that he would not be heard from for several days, it was the brilliant stroke of a master mind. Vicksburg was the greatest surrender of generals, of whom there were fifteen, and of armament and men that had ever been made since time began. This was an achievement of General Grant; but Gettysburg, on the other hand, was conspicuously a soldiers' battle.

CHAPTER XIII

Christian Endeavor Camp-fire

ARMORY, SATURDAY EVENING

SOMETHING new in a Convention program. All that was known about it was that the irrepressible William Shaw was to preside, and that "fagots from all parts of the world" were expected to be cast on the fire. It is doubtful if even Mr. Shaw knew just what he meant to do, — save that he intended to have some relaxation for a tired and faithful crowd, if one came. Whether anybody would come on a Saturday night, after an exhausting week, nobody could predict. But come they did, more than nine thousand of them, to see what it was all about. For one thing, it was about two hours, and two of the jolliest and most enjoyable of hours. The leader has the happy faculty of making everybody feel at home. He is a master of managing assemblies, and knows how to inject fun and enthusiasm. His first words set the pace. "We want to have a hot time in the old town tonight, if you will allow me to say it without seeming irreverent." That was a good beginning to get attention. He said he was there to pile the shavings together and put on the logs and get the fire to going. But after the devotional services, which had plenty of ringing hymns, he kindled a real blaze by a forceful, straight-out talk that made some homely truths known. He said he had been asked to repeat a statement he had made the day before, and he would gladly do so. Here it is, for everybody should read it: —

> Since the United Society publishing department was organized in 1889 no society has contributed a penny for the running expenses of the movement, but everything that has been needed — the salary of the general secretary and the literature that has been distributed — has all been paid for from the profits of the publishing concern.
>
> In all the twenty-five years since the Christian Endeavor movement was started, Dr. Clark has never received one dollar from the society for salary or personal expenses.
>
> Some people have hinted that they would like to go around the world and have their expenses paid by the United Society. It is a good thing for those people to know that Dr. Clark has traveled more than 400,000 miles in the interest of Christian Endeavor, and never once have his expenses been paid by the United Society. When they have not been paid by the conventions to which he has gone, he has paid them himself by his pen.

He was interrupted here by tremendous applause, and when it subsided he continued: —

That statement is always received with applause, and I begin to wonder why — whether it is for Dr. Clark's self-sacrifice or our own meanness. For, of all men, I wonder most why Dr. Clark should have to spend his days earning his own living, that he may help other people, and I begin to feel it is time for us to stop glorying in his self-sacrifice and get in a little on our own account.

I had a letter from Dr. Clark to-day in which he said that he had learned from the papers that a $2,000,000 building was planned that was to be a memorial to him. He said he did not want any memorial and he don't. But we ought to see that he has one.

As a matter of fact, the cost of the building we hope to have has not entered into our plans. We believed that the young people would give a silver quarter — that is, one cent a year for each year of the existence of the Society — for our silver anniversary, and with that a "suitable" building should be erected which would serve as our headquarters and would also be a memorial to Dr. Clark. If any money were left after the erection of the building our idea was that it should be used in furthering the young people's work in all the world.

Dr. Clark earns his own living, and he is going to continue to earn it.

How many salaried officers has the United Society? It has now, and has had in the past, just one paid officer — a general secretary who keeps in touch with the 67,000 separate Christian Endeavor societies. I have made the assertion before at this Convention — and I repeat it — there is no organization in the world that is doing such work as the Christian Endeavor, and that is practically — yes, fully — earning its own living. In the twenty-two years since I have been doing Christian Endeavor work — I am an old "mossback" in Christian Endeavor — I have never received one penny from the United Society. Nobody is getting rich on the Christian Endeavor movement, I can tell you that.

All along through this glowing reply to carping critics, the points were greeted with loud applause, and at the close he received an ovation.

"The world for Christ," he said before he introduced the others who were to help make the camp-fire blaze, "is the motto of our Society. Here we have it before us in the glowing electric lights. I believe we are near the power house here from which will go the influence to make Christ and Him crucified glow in the lives of the young people the world around."

Mr. Randall, of Jamaica, was the first man whom Mr. Shaw called out. He promised the co-operation of Jamaica Endeavorers, for the quarter-century fund. He also urged the Endeavorers, while giving their quarters, not to fail to stir up those that can afford to give larger sums.

Then Mr. Atwood, chairman of the Committee of 1905, was introduced to give a few notices, and received a hearty welcome, as he deserved. It was the birthday of Mr. Gilligan, the efficient head of the Convention Press Committee, and he was called to the platform to receive a written message of gratitude signed by many of the reporters and editors present.

Mr. Don O. Shelton, next called out, urged the quarter-century memorial fund for three reasons: because the Christian Endeavor office, by its sunshiny, optimistic letters, is a center of cheer for the whole country; because this Christian Endeavor movement has been closely allied through all its history to the missionary interests of the church; and because that model young people's paper, the *Christian*

Endeavor World, which is a power for righteousness, ought to be in a permanent home. Every speaker was generously applauded, for the fire was burning brightly.

Then Professor Wells, who makes the paper Mr. Shelton rightly praised, was unexpectedly called on for his fagot: He paid an affectionate tribute to Dr. Clark for his devotion and self-sacrifice in the cause of the Christian Endeavor. He said he had been asked dozens of times since the Convention began, "What is the matter with Dr. Clark?" "I'll tell you what it is," he said, answering the query, "his disease is overwork — simply that and nothing else. I have seen him spending himself all these years, and, if this continues, his precious life will not last as long as it ought. Not one thought of himself has entered into anything he has done in all these twenty-five years. I believe that this movement for this anniversary offering should be made unanimous by every society. Not here, but after you go home, so that it can be ratified by every member in your societies. So I want to give you this as your motto: 'A quarter apiece for Christian Endeavor headquarters, and no quarter until you give it.'"

Then came another of those exciting and dramatic scenes such as marked the Junior Rally. It was during the singing of the stirrring piece, "The Stars and Stripes Forever." At the chorus the choir flung out suddenly hundreds of flags which they waved in time with the music. The audience flung out their handkerchiefs and waved them above their heads back and forth in time. Then they applauded till the choir sung the piece again. Once more the applause insisted, and this time the enthusiasm redoubled as Baltimore's own song, "The Star-Spangled Banner," was given. Christian Endeavor no longer enthusiastic? Well!

Mr. Shaw had the happy thought, as he looked over the audience, to call upon all the men to rise, while the women remained seated. Instantly the entire Armory was changed in color from white to black, so many men responded. "They say men are not interested in religion and don't go to church," said Mr. Shaw satirically; whereupon everybody laughed and then cheered, as the refutation had been so complete of a common slander on the men.

Three more speakers were called out, each representing an Asiatic country, — Mr. Ogawa, who wished us *Banzai*, — ten thousand years for Christian Endeavor and the United Society; Dr. Hallock, who appeared in an interesting Chinese garb, and urged the quarter-century fund for the sake of what it would do for China; and Dr. Hume, who made the same plea for the sake of India.

Much appreciation was shown of a telegram received in reply to the telegram which the Convention authorized its officers to send to the Epworth League Convention in Denver. This reply was: —

The Seventh International Convention of Epworth Leagues greets you in the Spirit of our common Lord.

STEPHEN J. HERBEN.

At the close of what was a most hilarious evening, Mr. Shaw evoked some hilarious giving for the cause of Christian Endeavor's foreign work already undertaken, — a work that must in some way be supported, to the tune of $10,000 a year, while we are engaged in raising the quarter-century fund. Then the meeting was turned into a general buzz of greetings and hand-shakings, and the Endeavorers were loth to leave the hall.

The Christian Endeavor Camp-fire has come to stay in the International program. Tired and hot, but happy and jubilant, the delegates turned to their places of rest.

CHAPTER XIV

The Sunday Services

TERRIFIC was the heat on Sunday, exceeding even that on the preceding days. The heavy rains had ceased, and perhaps the humidity had decreased slightly, but the mercury had risen until it was a baking, broiling day. Christian Endeavor was in possession of Baltimore, however, including the pulpits, and everywhere on the streets were to be seen the delegates making their way to the morning worship. Seventy-seven of the evangelical churches of the city of churches opened their pulpits to the representatives of Christian Endeavor, and more pulpits would have been occupied in this way had there been more preachers available. Reports from the preachers showed an extraordinary attendance, despite the heat, and the churches will not forget the visitors who proclaimed the gospel. The reception was most cordial from the church members, and again Baltimore made manifest the delightful courtesy and cordiality which give her deservedly high place as a host. Here is a characteristic episode that came within the writer's notice.

In one church, at the close of the service, it seemed as though the entire congregation, men, women, and children, tarried to give the Christian Endeavor preacher greeting. It was an informal reception of charming kind. Toward the close of it a courtly gentleman with white hair said to the preacher, after looking intently at him, "You are a Marylander, sir?" as though he had settled that point to his satisfaction. "No," was the reply, I happen to be a New Yorker." "Well," was the unexpected response, "that is strange; I didn't know they raised such fine looking men as you in the North. But you can preach all right, sir, and I hope you'll come this way often." A hope that was echoed in the preacher's heart, while those standing near-by were smiling broadly at the sincere but left-handed compliment.

THE CONSECRATION MEETINGS

In the evening there were twenty-one simultaneous consecration meetings in as many churches, covering all sections of the city, "from Dan to Beersheba," as one pastor on the outskirts said. There was also a general·meeting at Lyric Hall in the interest of reforms. To particularize as to all these meetings would clearly be beyond our space limits. It can only be said, in general, that the reports from all these meetings were similar in tone — churches full or well filled with interested audiences;

strong addresses by leading Endeavor workers; a reaching of the members of the churches of the city such as could have been accomplished in no other way. It is worthy of note that in four of the largest churches the subject of missions, home and foreign, was made the distinctive feature, with addresses by Mr. Hicks and Mr. Shelton, Missionaries Knipp of Japan, Hallock of China, and Hume of India, Miss Stone, Mr. C. Ogawa, and Rev. Jiro Abratani of Japan, Miss Evanka Akrabova of Bulgaria, Dr. Hatch and Dr. Goucher of the Woman's College, Baltimore.

Here are samples simply from reports kindly furnished, of what was said at these meetings, the consecration part of which was conducted in nearly all cases by the presidents of State unions: —

At the North United Presbyterian Church, Miss E. Stafford Millar, of Australia, gave one of the most impressive addresses of the Convention. With a winning and magnetic personality, she held her hearers intent. Men leaned forward in their pews, women forgot the discomforts of the heat, as they learned the secret of true success. "The experienced traveler carries little baggage. Many professed Christians weigh themselves down with all sorts of useless luggage. Everything that hinders must be cast aside."

Dr. Hallenbeck, at the Waverly Presbyterian Church: A single soul is worth the toil and sacrifice of threescore years and ten. Not all can be preachers, but all can be soul winners. The net method of fishing for souls is the exceptional; most gospel fishing is by hook. There can be no genuine revival without personal work, without a faithful witnessing.

Dr. Landrith, at Babcock Memorial: Theme, the Changeless Christ. There are two great eternities, yesterday and to-morrow, separated by a fleeting to-day. The astronomy of yesterday is the astrology of to-day. Changes in time are constant. We long for that which abides, and find it in Christ. What He said on earth two thousand years ago, He said for 1905.

Rev. George W. Collock, president of Virginia Union, leading consecration service, referring to fact that the church was a memorial to Dr. Maltbie D. Babcock, said: On the fly-leaf of his Bible after his death were found these words: "Committed myself again, without reservation, with Christian brothers, to unreserved docility and devotion before my Master."

At Abbott Memorial Presbyterian Church, Dr. Wynne Jones expressed thanks that the Convention arrangements had included a meeting in his church, which was far from the center. He said: The Convention is proving to be for the glory of God, the salvation of souls, the upbuilding of the church, and is making a deep impress on the city. Dr. Philputt, the speaker of the evening, said the pastor's feeling of "a power going out and coming in that is peculiar to this Convention is also the estimate of keen convention-goers and observers." "Where there is no depth of conviction there is no fervency of spirit."

President King, of Oberlin, at Mount Vernon Place Methodist Episcopal Church: No friendship is so much a matter of conscious arrangement as of unconscious growth. Any friendship needs expression. In no friendship is it wise for us to expect continuous emotion. Friendship grows most of all through continuous association. His theme was "Deepening Acquaintance with God."

At the consecration service in this church, Mr. John R. Clements, Secretary of the New York Union, told the Northfield experience of Dr. Babcock, when he was led to definite surrender for soul-winning labors, and also the story of Hugh McAlester Beaver, when out of a quiet hour experience he was led to a definite surrender for specific effort. Definite surrender for service was the keynote of the service.

Bishop J. S. Mills, at Otterbein United Brethren Church: Christian Endeavor is the spontaneous uprising of the young people, asking the churches to give them something to do. He heartily endorsed the federation of the United Brethren, Methodist Protestants, and Congregationalists.

William Shaw, at Trinity African Methodist Episcopal Church: When I meet our red Endeavorers among the Indians, our yellow ones among the Chinese, our browns in the Philippines, our bronze in India, our whites in Europe, and our blacks in America, I am happy to see that in all colors they are the best that God has made of every kind.

Rev. I. M. D. Gordon, native colored minister of Jamaica, at same meeting: I came to Baltimore as a pilgrim, but not as the Indian makes his pilgrimage to a shrine, to die there, but I came to Baltimore to get new life.

Missionary Meeting at Associate Congregational Church, as reported by President William R. Hassell, of Brooklyn Union, condensed: Church doubly perfect in its appointments at this service; spirit enthusastic, interest deep, attention devout; prayerfulness the keynote. Mr. Hicks quiet, convincing of argument and winning. "Give people a distinct call and they will respond." "Passion for Christian work rewards preparation through prayer." Dr. Hume of India: "Christian Missions are the Christian interpretation of God's commands." "If we are not believers in missions we should keep quiet every time the Lord's Prayer is repeated, for it is a mission prayer." As the consecration leader, Mr. Hassell, made his plea for immediate decision and consecration, there is reason to believe a number decided for Christ.

At Light Street Presbyterian Church, Rev. Jiro Abratani, of Japan, said: The doors are open to Christian education. High officials are now giving liberally to the Christian work among the soldiers. If we want to evangelize the Far East we must reach it through Japan.

Missionary Knipp of Japan, related the story of the young Japanese who, asked what he expected to do after leaving Japanese schools, said, "If health permits I will go to America to complete my education; then I want to establish in China a Christian school as Neesima did in Japan." When Japanese become Christians they are as loyal and faithful as any people in the world.

Don O. Shelton, at Brantly Baptist Church: As America goes forward into this new century, what is its greatest need? Is it not a largely increased number of Christian young men and women who possess, as their dominant, commanding purpose, the purpose that controlled the noble company of pioneer heroes of the cross, namely, the implicit doing of the will of Jesus Christ? The Church of Christ in America does not lack financial ability. To each individual Christian in America the Lord has intrusted personally a great and glorious task — the taking of the gospel to every creature in America.

Rev. Charles Stelzle at Second Presbyterian Church: Either we must admit that the church is equal to the problem of winning working men, or confess that in this generation it is a failure. The church can reach working men if it will go at the task with enthusiasm.

When the average church becomes impressed with its duty in this respect it will organize a little mission and place in charge of it a man, to whom it will pay six hundred dollars a year, and then expect him to solve problems that would stagger many a six thousand dollar man. We need our very best blood, our very best enthusiasm, in these down-town fields. Here, under proper leadership, our young people will find an opportunity for the employment of every talent, and in this altruistic age thousands of them stand ready to lay down their lives alongside of their less fortunate brothers; but the church hasn't given them the chance. Going into the work with the same spirit and devotion that we find in the foreign missionary, we shall begin a crusade for city missions that shall tell upon our great centers of population.

George B. Stewart, D.D., LL.D.

Rev. C. H. Hubbell

President Henry Churchill King

Rev. Oliver Huckel

Secretary Harry Wade Hicks

Secretary Don O. Shelton

CHAPTER XV

The Men's Meeting

AT THE ARMORY, SUNDAY AFTERNOON

This was in its line the most remarkable session of the Convention, and of any Endeavor convention. More than that, it was one of the most remarkable meetings purely for men that has ever been held. It reminded one of the Moody meetings for men. Rarely in the best days of that great evangelist did he gather from five to six thousand men together. That was what was done in Baltimore, on a Sunday afternoon when the sun was wilting and not a breath of air stirring. Had the conditions been more propitious, it is probable that the Armory would have been filled. Thousands of tickets of invitation had been given out, with special effort to reach the working men and the unconverted. When a show of hands was called for, that it might be known how large a proportion of those present was Christian, the result indicated that about one third of the number was not professedly Christian. It was evident, also, that fully half of the audience was made up of working men. At the suggestion of the leader, Dr. Hallenbeck, in consideration of the excessive heat, the men generally took off their coats, presenting the novel spectacle of a shirt-waist congregation. Fans bearing the C. E. monogram were given to every one present, and their motion made a buzzing sound louder than that of the electric fans. There was plenty of enthusiasm as the session got under way, but this deepened into intense seriousness as the evangelist, Mr. Biederwolf, who in his power over an audience approaches Mr. Moody more nearly than any evangelist now in service, made his powerful appeal. The reaching effect of the gospel, when faithfully and plainly and courageously and convictingly presented, has rarely been witnessed in greater measure. That was what made it a meeting to be remembered. It put the stamp and seal on the evangelistic character of the Convention, a character marked throughout.

The music was beautiful and most helpful. Over half of the great choir was present, and in addition, there was an excellent brass band and a cornet soloist, and Mr. Jacobs, with his rendering of gospel hymns, completed the spiritual effect musically. Then there was an unusual feature, for an Endeavor convention, in the taking of an offering to defray the expenses of the meeting. In announcing this, Mr. Shaw said it was at the request of the men themselves. He drew great applause from the men when he said that the working man is independent. He does not want pity, sympathy, or charity, all he asks is fair play, a chance, and a square deal, and he will pay his own bills. The response was generous as was the applause.

There were two addresses. First came Rev. Mr. Stelzle, of Chicago, who was a working man, was converted and led into the ministry, and is devoting his life to bringing the church into right relations with men who feel that the church is not for them. The church for the working man was the burden of his address, which was quiet and practical, attempting to convince the judgment rather than move the emotions. He said in part: —

There are twenty-six million Protestants and Catholics in this country, and among that number there must be many working men. Frankly and fearlessly I want to say that it is not true the rich are the representatives of the church of Jesus Christ. We hear so much about ten thousand dollar contributions that we are believing that the church is being supported entirely by such contributions, but in fact the church is supported by the small gifts of the many.

The church that the working man is supporting is not the church of the rich, but the church of his mother, who taught him the inspiration that he needs in his darkest hours. It has been said that the church is opposed to the working man. Jesus Christ never said that the church was opposed to the working man. Christ is the head of the church, and we look to Him for its teachings.

His church was made up of working men, working men listened to him and came from all places to hear the priceless words that came from His lips. The Apostles were working men, and they were not opposed to them. They were surely the church of the working man.

The prophets of the church are not opposed to working men. The text-book of the church is the Bible, and the Bible is not opposed to the working men. It is the working men's book, and if its principles were followed out they would solve the great social questions of the present.

The Bible is the only text-book that is officially recognized by the church, and it is up-to-date on all social questions. The Bible is always up-to-date because it came from God. Thousands and thousands of working men laid down their lives in the early history of the church for its principles.

The majority of ministers are not opposed to the working man, and I have met and talked with more ministers, I dare say, than any other minister. I went to a meeting of labor editors and found out that most of them were members of church.

I have met several presidents of national labor unions in the United States, and they were all church officers. If the church is opposed to the working man and would not welcome them, would labor union leaders be in it? The tie is very much in common between the church and labor unions.

Mr. Stelzle then read a pledge that every man has to sign when joining the American Federation of Labor, and said that in it a high standard hard to meet was set and the principles of Christianity were embodied in it.

"The church needs the working men," concluded the speaker. "Jesus Christ wants them and the working men need the church. They think they don't need the church, but they are mistaken, for they do."

These statements met with hearty response. What was said about the leaders of labor movements was undoubtedly a surprise to the audience. It should be widely known, as an answer to the common statement that the working men are thoroughly apart from and hostile to the church.

The cornet solo that followed was wonderfully sweet, telling out a gospel story so effectively that another was demanded. Then Dr. Hallenbeck placed the meeting in the charge of Rev. William E. Biederwolf, of Indiana, a Presbyterian minister who is Mr. Chapman's strongest speaker in the evangelistic campaign which the Presbyterian denomination is carrying on so determinedly and successfully.

Mr. Biederwolf has a personality that tells. He is a tall, wholesome, manly, clear-eyed, whole-souled man — man every inch of him. He is good-looking in Emerson's definition of it, "looking good." He is in dead earnest, but not one of the emotional type. He appeals to the mind as well as the heart. He does not seek to stir the surface but to impel the soul from its depths. He is a master of rapid, straightforward, direct, terse, and picturesque English style. He never stops at the end of a paragraph, but has you going on the new tack before you know it. Rapid, he is distinct in enunciation; with a voice ringing and carrying far; with a manner familiar yet dignified. The whole man was in that speech. It was a direct effort to bring lost men to God through the preaching of the plain truth. And how it went home! Not only those who had no church membership were hit by those sharp strokes. Every man there felt his sinfulness, and knew that charity became him and humility and penitence. Cumulatively it flowed along until the stream of eloquence burst the banks, and under the passionate appeal for a white life, for the sake of mother, children, society, above all, for the sake of Christ the Saviour, strong men wept and bent their heads and then rose and went forward in confession of sin and desire for a better life.

The writer has been with Mr. Moody through many revivals, from the great days in Chicago on, but has heard no more convincing and courageous and stirring sermon than this, nor seen more immediate and striking results. No report can give the power of such an address, but here are some things that will indicate its line. He read the lament of David over his son Absalom, and took Absalom as his illustration of a wrecked and wasted life, brilliant in promise and opportunity. He said: —

> Absalom was living a high life. High life leads to fast life; fast life is the macadamized road to hell. Life is a battle, and there is no room for brainless dudes. It takes a man to fight it. It's a great thing to be a man. A man is the best that God can do. He is not always the man we see to-day, for he oftentimes is but little better than the little boy's definition of a man — "An animal split at one end that walks on the split end."
>
> The young individual with the high collar and a cane thinks he is a man, and that the most correct way to let the public know it is to smoke a cigarette and punch a pool ball. But you are not a man. You are a cipher with the rim left off. This kind finds his chief joy in the wine-room, at the gaming table and in conversation with lewd women, and he will find himself enervated for the struggle and defeated in the battle.
>
> Knowledge and fine physique alone do not make a man. Something else must run through a man's makeup before he can be worthy of the name; and that is a strong vein of the spiritual. The image stamped upon man at the beginning was a moral likeness to God. Animals have minds and beasts have bodies and they use them to take care of themselves as best they can; but man has a soul. He is a soul, and for a human being to cultivate the body and care for the mind and neglect the soul is to be less of a man than a beast is an animal. That individual is the real man, who realizes that he is the handiwork of God, body, mind and soul, and tries to honor his Maker in every department of his being. And there's nothing more unspeakably sad than to see a human being created in the image of his God giving himself up to that which is vile and unholy, galloping possibly through a course of revelry and nastiness, and then, when the end is come, have

nothing left for God but the dregs of a wasted life, which are laid at his feet with a miserable whine for mercy.

Mr. Biederwolf then proceeded to review the sins that are common to man, as Sabbath-breaking, intemperance, gambling, profanity, lust, impure reading and imagination. His pictures were startlingly vivid. He said that a man who used God's seventh and sacred day in a way to please himself, after God had already given him six days in which to do work and pleasure, was like the man who steals a man's seventh and last dollar when the man had already given him six.

He pleaded with the intemperate man and scored the gambler. He said that a gambler was the meanest, lowest, and most contemptible thing that passed for man, and of all things that draw breath under the sun. He said that the man who was given to profanity, and made no attempt to cease from it, was low grain in his fiber and not a gentleman. He paused, and said, "You are not having any trouble to understand me, are you?"

When the speaker came to the sin of impurity he spoke of the foul-hearted libertine in words that burned and stung. He scored the double standard of morals, and declared there should be only one. This was strongly applauded. Concerning the sins of the imagination, he said, "Think well, and do well will follow thought."

Impure language, he said, will spread contagion worse than smallpox, and that the man who believes in a higher standard of purity for his wife and sister than for himself deserves to be boycotted by decent and respectable society.

He closed with five reasons why every man in the audience should begin the "White Life," which he showed to be the Christian Life. These reasons are — because the Christian life is the only manly life, the only reasonable life, a life of great blessing, the only heavenly kind of life, and because others in the home and elsewhere need the help that can be gained from one who leads such a life.

Then came an intense appeal for men to show by rising that they would enter the Christian life and that they wanted the prayers of Christians. One man rose, another, several in different places. They remained standing but a few moments, but there was a steady succession until scores would be on their feet at once in all parts of the hall. Mr. Jacobs uttered in song a tender and appealing prayer. The evangelist, standing on a table to gain more commanding position, put all his energy into a last appeal to do the right and manly thing, and then asked all who had risen to come forward and stand while prayer was offered for them, while hundreds of hands went up from those that wished prayer to be offered for friends. Christian workers had been supplied with cards that were circulated for signature by those that had decided for Christ. Meantime, Mr. Biederwolf and others were passing around, grasping the hands of those that had taken the stand, between three and four hundred in all, many of whom were deeply moved and in tears. As the great crowd gradually passed out from this wonderfully blessed meeting, the choir softly sang, "God be with you till we meet again."

Of this meeting, the results of which came as a surprise to nearly everybody, the *Christian Endeavor World* rightly says: "There were, during the Convention, sessions of inspiration and of instruction that will bear fruit in hundreds of societies throughout the coming year, but there was one meeting above all others that ended in immediate results of the most blessed kind. It was a meeting unequaled by any that had ever been held in Baltimore; it was a meeting surpassing in its effects any connected with previous conventions; it was the most important meeting at Baltimore."

CHAPTER XVI

The Woman's Meeting

LYRIC HALL, SUNDAY AFTERNOON

THE Woman's Meeting has evidently become a permanent feature of our conventions. At first it seemed to be held in order that the women might have somewhere to go while the *real* meetings of the Convention, for men and for boys and girls, were in session. But it has been proven that Christian women find great help and inspiration in meeting together, strengthening one another's faith, and tacitly covenanting together to uphold the standards that they love.

On Sunday afternoon Lyric Hall was filled in every part, including the galleries, the boxes, and the platform, while many women who could not obtain seats were content to stand in the aisles at the sides of the hall. The gracious leader of music, Mr. R. A. Harris, with real Southern gallantry said, as he faced the company, nearly all of whom were dressed in white, "This is certainly a very fair audience."

Mrs. Clark was to have presided at the meeting, but the sickness of Dr. Clark caused her to relinquish all her plans for the Convention. Mrs. James L. Hill, of Salem, Mass., one of the foremost Junior workers in America, and a most accomplished leader, had been appointed to preside in Mrs. Clark's absence. She said at the opening of the service, "I do not for a moment assume to be taking Mrs. Clark's place. One person can never take another's person place. A person can only take her own place, and my place to-day is that of an emergency woman." She proved that Christian Endeavor's "emergency" type would take high rank as a regular in any organization. She read a message from Mrs. Clark, which met with hearty applause. It was as follows: —

> I am glad to send my greetings through you to the Woman's Meeting on Sunday afternoon. I cannot tell you how sorry I shall be not to be there. I shall miss all the inspiration that comes from looking into the faces of that great company of Christian women and feeling that we are all working together for the Master, whose we are and whom we serve. I shall miss all the helpful words that I am sure you will have from the speakers of the day, though I shall get what comfort I can from the newspaper reports. I shall be with you in spirit. "I also helping together by prayer." May it be one of the best meetings of the Convention, and may it generate such a spirit of earnest enthusiasm as shall lead all who are present to do a larger and better work for the Master in all the coming months because of the help and inspiration there received.
>
> With cordial greetings from us both to all our fellow workers who may happen to inquire for us, affectionately and gratefully yours,
>
> HARRIET A. CLARK.

The audience unanimously voted to send in response this telegram to Mrs. Clark:—

BALTIMORE, July 9, 1905.
Thirty-four hundred women, assembled in Lyric Hall for worship and inspiration, send Mrs. Clark affectionate salutations, love, all good wishes, and assurances of appreciation, gratitude, and prayer.

The devotions, led by Miss Evanka Akrabova, of Philippopolis, Bulgaria, formed an object lesson in missions, showing what spiritual and religious development can be brought to persons who receive the blessed Gospel.

Miss Ellen M. Stone, received with the flutter of thousands of handkerchiefs, told in her own inimitable manner the wonderful story of the way in which the Lord had led her, while there seemed to be not so much as the turning of an eye, so closely did every one listen to her address.

Miss E. Stafford Millar, of Australia, had great power and magnetism. Whether in singing, in bowing the head in prayer, or in simply listening, the women were glad to grant her slightest wish. She was strongly evangelistic, and thus voiced the sentiment of the company present. She even seemed like a prophetess, with her impassioned utterances, her tall willowy figure, her long clinging dress with its loose sleeves, falling from her arms as she made her strong effective gestures. Some one said that she looked like Sargent's pictures of the prophets in the Boston Public Library. The religious fervor was even heightened by the solos by Miss Grace Beelman, of Dayton, Ohio, upon her eloquent cornet, for it seemed to speak words of tender invitation and entreaty. The Misses Maya Das sang greetings from India in their native language.

This meeting made one grateful for all the Christian womanhood that is allied with our blessed cause, and devoutly thankful that in this day of the New Woman, with the hundreds of open doors before her, which lead to pleasure, to wealth and to fame, there were, assembled in one place, thousands of women (many of them young and talented) who love nothing better than to worship God in the beauty of holiness.

BATTLE MONUMENT

BATTLE MONUMENT AND COURT HOUSE

CHAPTER XVII

The Boys' and Girls' Meeting

ASSOCIATE CHURCH, SUNDAY AFTERNOON

It was to be expected, after the Junior Rally and the various Junior and Intermediate meetings and receptions, that the Sunday afternoon meeting of the children would be a great event. So it was for the thousand children and sprinkling of older "children" who filled the beautiful Associate Church. What a congregation of sweet-faced, eager, happy children it was. Certainly Rev. Carey Bonner, who was to give them one of the most delightful hours of their lives, never faced a more bewitching company, or had closer attention. Happy he was, too, for if he knows how to conduct a great chorus, he is equally apt at talking to children. His "Sunshine Talk" was a model. The session was the "gem" session of the Convention.

The gathering was presided over by Miss Margaret Koch, while Mr. Foster, who is at home with the children, and who looked cool as the coolest in his suit of pure white, led the singing. Miss Emma Post, of Baltimore, and Professor Wells, whose heart takes in all the children, also took part. The Misses Maya Das, of India, sang several religious songs in their native language. One was the translation of "Jesus loves me, this I know," which was recognized by the tune. They wore dresses of a sober light brown shade and had deep red shawls over their heads. One of them is studying medicine in Philadelphia and the other is attending Mount Holyoke College.

However, Rev. Mr. Bonner and the white-frocked girls and white-shirtwaisted boys were the real performers. Mr. Bonner talked ideas, and his listeners repeated them in song.

"I don't believe in telling them too much," he said after the meeting. "Tell them one idea, or give them one line of thought and make them remember it." And that assuredly he did. That silver-lining verse will brighten many a dark day.

Mr. Bonner, who may be called a child-fascinator, was enthusiastically received. He instantly attracted the attention of all, and never lost it from that moment. He pulled a cord and drew a sheet down across the arch back of the pulpit. On it was printed Miss Ellen T. Fowler's stanza: —

> "The inner side of every cloud
>   Is bright and shining;
> I therefore turn my clouds about
> And always wear them inside out
>   To show the lining."

Mr. Bonner sat down at the piano, and played a little tune for the stanza, which the children learned immediately. Then the kindly-faced Englishman told the story of the two buckets. One of them wore his clouds cloud-side out, and whined, "No matter how much water I bring up from the well, I always come back empty." The other wore his clouds the bright side out, and cheerily said, "No matter how often I come to the well empty, I always go away full of water for thirsty souls."

Mr. Bonner told of Paul and Silas, turning their clouds about and singing in prison. He told about two little children in a London slum. The boy had got hold of an old overcoat with a fur lining, and was strutting around with the fur side out. The girl had turned an old, red-lined cloak inside out, and was very grand in it. "Who are you?" they were asked. "I'm the Queen of Hingland," said the girl. Said the boy, "I'm the bloomin' Duke of York, that's what I am."

In illustration of clouds and their lining, Mr. Bonner did some sums. Banners were held up by long wands in the hands of Junior girls, and were unrolled by Mr. Bonner, line by line, the lines being read in concert by the children. The first banner, in black letters with a black border, read, line below line: "Sulks," "Grumbles," "Blues," "Frowns"; then a line, and the total was "Gloomy Selfishness." In the same way the opposites were shown in gilded letters: "Love," "Good Temper," "A Merry Heart," "Smiles," and the total, "Glad Service."

Then came an illustration from grammar. "How many degrees of comparison are there?" Promptly came the answer from the well-taught children, "Positive, Comparative, Superlative." More banners were displayed: —

> Positive — Sulks are no good (in black).
> Comparative — Dimples are better than dumps (in blue).
> Superlative — God's sunshine is best (in gilt).

Then the boys had an exercise in grammar. They showed a banner, in red letters, in the imperative mood: "Catch the sunshine." How are we to do it? Mr. Bonner told of a little boy whom he saw once, sitting in a flood of sunlight. The little fellow stretched out both his hands, clasped them to his breast, and cried, "*My* sunshine!" Mr. Bonner had the Juniors do the same thing.

A bit of gymnastics followed, one of the boys swinging forward the rest of the banner, which had been doubled back behind. Then the banner read, "Catch the sunshine: and pass it on."

How can we do this? Mr. Bonner took a mirror from his pocket. "Every boy or girl," he said, "is God's mirror; but if I put the mirror in my pocket or in a dark cellar, it's no good. Where are we to be, if we would catch the sunshine? Now for a lesson in geography." The boys and girls who had been helping Mr. Bonner repeated in concert: "Then spake Jesus unto them, saying, I am the light of the world, and he that followeth me shall not walk in darkness." The last of the banners was then displayed, the two words in scarlet, "Follow Me." That is where we may catch the sunshine and pass it on.

It was with new sense of their beauty and force that we sung once more Miss Fowler's verse, each section of the audience singing it separately, and then all together. A simple prayer, and "There's sunshine in my soul," brought to a close one of the sweetest and most effective children's services ever conducted. It takes a genius to originate and conduct such an exercise. It is too bad Mr. Bonner does not live in America all the time. What a Junior Endeavor Secretary he would make, and what a flood of sunshine he would bring into American child life.

CHAPTER XVIII

Two Great Reforms

LYRIC HALL, SUNDAY EVENING

TEMPERANCE and Sabbath Desecration, or the duty to preserve the American and Christian Sunday, were the two great reform ideas brought forward eloquently and forcibly before an audience that thronged Lyric Hall for the second time this hot Sunday. Another great session — that was the common verdict. Secretary Vogt presided happily. Christian Endeavor is rapidly developing him, and he has admirable executive and also presiding qualities. Those who remember how Endeavor "raised" John Willis Baer are observing the same process in the lovable successor to a much loved worker. How people like manliness!

Mr. Foster led the service of praise, Dr. MacMillan the devotions, and then Henry W. Wilbur, editor of the *Philanthropist* of Philadelphia, spoke on "Iniquity's Siamese Twins" — tobacco and whisky. Picturing the rapid pace of our modern life, Mr. Wilbur reminded us that the faster we move, the more terrific is the wreck if anything gets in our way. There are three factors in society's welfare, — moral integrity, intellectual ability, and industrial prosperity. Now every one of these factors is destroyed by the licensed drink traffic. The duty of the citizen toward this evil business is to turn the forces of government against it, instead of maintaining a partnership with it. "You may shout yourself hoarse for the flag, but until you dignify it with civic duty you have only dignified it as a rag."

The address was a powerful arraignment of the weak-kneed, indolent, careless voter. The Endeavorers applauded his stirring sentences with all their energy.

All Endeavorers know and honor Dr. Mary Wood-Allen, world's superintendent of the Purity Department of the Woman's Christian Temperance Union. "The Strength of Ten," from Sir Galahad, whose "strength was as the strength of ten because his heart was pure," — this was her theme. Her thoughtful and impressive talk was based on the wonderful power of inheritance. When Napoleon's marshals were taunted with their lack of pedigrees, they nobly answered, "We, we are ancestors." This thought must never be forgotten by those that would make the world better. The nations of the future are wrapped up in the young of to-day. For the sake of this world that is to come, she made a strong plea for personal purity. Here are a few of her telling sentences: —

"Blessed are the pure in heart, for they shall see God." When Sir Galahad attributed his strength to his purity of heart he was stating a scientific fact, as well as a poetical sentiment. Thoughts affect bodily conditions. Fear paralyzes and destroys strength; courage arouses strength; grief so abstracts the strength that the person may fall as if dead; joy will bring strength to limbs that were trembling and faint,

Each one of us is an Atlas, bearing the world on our individual shoulders. Surely, we need strength for such a burden. If we fail to stand erect in the stress of life, if we lose courage, if we lower our standards of conduct, the world sinks by so much. But if we are straight in life, upright in conduct, the world is raised to that much higher level. No matter how obscure you may think yourself, how little noted, you are moving the world by your thoughts as they crystalize into conduct. You young people are deciding to-day what shall be the attitude of the world in physical strength, in mental power, in moral greatness, for all the years to come. Do you not see what value you should set upon yourselves and upon your education? If we are the repositories of the virtues of the race, the earlier we begin the cultivation of those virtues in ourselves the better. An outside compliance with moral law is not enough. The virtue must be rooted in our thought.

First is the virtue of self-reverence. "What! Know ye not that your bodies are the temple of the Holy Ghost?" This thought sanctifies all bodily acts. Health becomes a sacred duty, and it behooves us to eat and drink as unto the Lord.

Our habits are not personal matters, but influence the race. The idea of the value of each individual to the race indicates the need of reverence of the manhood and womanhood of others, for they are also potential ancestors. The little boy and the child-woman are not to be treated as of no importance. In truth they are important members of society. A wrong to one of them is a wrong to the race.

"I am sure," said Secretary Vogt, "that we do not half understand how far a man may be legislated into the Kingdom." This he said in introducing Dr. R. C. Wylie, the treasurer of the National Reform Association, who spoke on "The Constitutional Basis of the American Sabbath." He told us that forty-three of our forty-five States have Sabbath laws, which have been declared constitutional by the State supreme courts wherever they have been tested. These Sabbath laws invade no one's rights; they protect the rights of all the people; they concern a civil institution, for that is what the Sabbath is, as well as a religious one; they concern the police power of the State; they are based on the divine law, which is recognized as authoritative by the statute law and the court opinions. Dr. Wylie has for years made a study of the law on this subject, and speaks from first-hand knowledge. He said: —

But we take a step in advance and declare that Sabbath laws are necessary for the protection of rights. Government is the institution of rights, and if it can be shown that Sabbath laws are necessary to protect human rights, such laws must have a good constitutional basis. Our courts declare that we have the right to rest one day in seven and spend it in the worship of God, if we so desire. Without Sabbath laws such rest is impossible. Multitudes of laborers have no Sabbath rest, not because they prefer working seven days in the week, but because they must or give up their positions. Many capitalists feel compelled by the laws of competition to carry on their business continuously, although they prefer to rest one day in seven. Of these facts our courts have often taken notice and sustain rest-day laws accordingly.

Sabbath laws are police regulations, designed for the public welfare. The police power of the state is that power whereby it may protect the public health, peace, and morals. Without a discordant note our courts declare that Sabbath laws accomplish these ends. Either of them is sufficient to justify such legislation, but the matter of public morals should receive special mention. No free government can exist without a moral citizenship. Time for the cultivation of morals is a necessary condition of morality among the people. The outcry against Sabbath laws as an infringement upon liberty is the outcry of anarchy or tyranny. The freest lands under heaven are those with the strictest Sabbath laws. Sabbath laws are grounded in the will of God.

This is one of the important subjects demanding attention to-day. The working men are losing their Sabbath. Sunday laws are unblushingly violated. Conscience has indeed taken a fearful slump, as Dr. Gladden would say, on this question. We need a bracing up. Secretary Vogt introduced Dr. Samuel McNaugher, of Boston, a Trustee of the United Society, to speak on "The Attitude of the Individual American to the Sabbath." Among other things he said: —

On one occasion a young prince of India, when on a visit to England, asked Queen Victoria the reason of England's greatness. Whereupon the good and great Queen pointed to the open Bible and said, "The open Bible is the cause of England's greatness." In like manner people in all parts of the world are asking what is the cause of America's greatness. Immigrants are coming to us from all parts of Europe and Asia and Africa, because of what they have seen and heard abroad of this country. The character of this immigration has changed greatly during the past ten years as the center of this movement has gone from the parallel of Berlin to that of Constantinople. We are all aware of what that means. These people come to us and desire that our institutions be changed. They make this demand in their ignorance. Many of our corrupt politicians are making use of this in order to secure votes, and we are told that we must give the foreigner a continental Sunday.

Certainly this is wrong, and those of us who have been born in this country ought to stand for God and for his Word as the only national safeguard. The Sabbath has had its great place in our national life, and if we lose it, then will come a condition like that which we now find in these other countries.

1. The Sabbath day, rightly observed, will bring a blessing to any people.
2. Our national perpetuity and greatness is included in this question of the Sabbath.
3. All of our American Christian institutions are being tested and the Sabbath very specially.
4. We should write into our national Constitution God's law on the Sabbath and thus teach all men the reason of our greatness and provide against any attack being made in the future.
5. If the Sabbath is abolished the Christian religion will be abolished with it. The question whether this day is to be observed or desecrated is just a question of life or death in regard to Christianity. Here is our individual patriotic duty.

The sentiment of the great audience regarding all these reform questions of the evening was never in doubt. It was a stimulating and backbone-stiffening meeting.

MONUMENT TO THE MARYLAND HEROES OF THE REVOLUTION

CHAPTER XIX

Recognition Morning

AT THE ARMORY, MONDAY

The closing day — last day of the feast, and by no means the least day. Sunshine, and hot sunshine, but less humidity if not less torridity. Baltimore Convention will be remembered as the best, the most dramatic in features, the wettest and the hottest and the happiest. But if you could poll the delegates, it is probable that ninety-nine and often the other one in every hundred would gladly go through the spell of weather again to attend such meetings.

Recognition Morning was a new feature on the program. The collective work in Societies and Unions was to be honored, with responses from many State and Local Union officers. Dr. Hill presided at this session, and Mr. Jacobs led the singing for the last time, as he was to return to New York in the afternoon. He must feel happy at the treatment accorded him by chorus and audiences, and he rendered most helpful service.

Enthusiasm bubbled over at this session. There was room for it. Nothing like it had gone before. The Camp Fire was informal and sociable, but this was joy and jollification over actual work done and rewards earned. Like the Camp Fire, Recognition Morning will hold its place in programs to be. The *Sun* described it as "a great and glowing spectacle of life and color."

The morning began with jollification. Preceding the opening of the meeting the delegations from the various States, especially those that are seeking the next convention, gathered in the auditorium and gave yells and sang songs. For many minutes the large hall rang with the din of hundreds of voices and enthusiasm ran at a high pitch.

Foremost in the shouting were the four cities that are fighting for the next convention — Kansas City, Minneapolis, Los Angeles, and Seattle — and they stood upon their chairs, and, with their banners waving far above their heads, they good-naturedly shouted back at each other. This scene was continued until Musical Director Jacobs stepped forward and called for silence.

As each delegation gathered together and took their seats they displayed pasteboard signs bearing the name of the State from which they came, and they held these high in the air, with the name facing the Hoffman street entrance, so that if any of the straggling delegates entered, they could easily locate their body of Endeavorers.

Dr. Hill said somebody once said that the Christian Endeavor Society was dead, but, if one had to judge from the remarkable demonstrations before him, there must have been a resurrection. He then stated that the meeting was on the order of the commencement exercises of a large school, and that he felt proud to deliver to the various delegates and the Unions the pamphlets, pennants, and banners in recognition of the great work they have accomplished since the last biennial convention.

In calling out the names and presenting the banners Dr. Hill was assisted by Secretary Vogt, who made many bright and encouraging remarks as he called out the names of the various States, cities, and districts that were presented with the pamphlets and certificates of recognition.

On the front of the platform were more than fifty chairs, heaped high with great bundles of envelopes. Each chairful was for a State, Territory, or Province. In the envelopes were the diplomas granted by the United Society for specially successful efforts along the five lines of devotional and evangelistic endeavor, committee activities, educational endeavor, Christian beneficence, and good-citizenship endeavor. There were also the beautiful Increase Certificates granted for an increase of at least 25 per cent in society membership, a charmingly designed and admirably printed certificate, bearing beautiful Christian Endeavor pictures from all parts of the world.

The envelopes also contained copies of the most remarkable document, next to the pledge, ever sent forth by Christian Endeavor, — "The Recognition Leaflet." "Leaflet" is too modest a term. It is a handsomely printed pamphlet of seventy pages. It contains about six thousand items. Each item stands for splendid and varied services.

Roll of Honor

The first to be called out were the societies that were worthy of recognition for devotional and evangelistic endeavor; Christian Endeavor committee activites; educational endeavor; Christian beneficence and good-citizenship endeavors. In the large pamphlet were incorporated the names of the States, the cities, and the names of the church. with the number of phases of work on which they were entitled to recognition.

There were 5,406 societies in this list; 1,605 of them had increased their membership over 25 per cent.; 3,196 received certificates for devotional and evangelistic endeavor; 1,305 for committee activities; 982 for educational endeavor; 1,731 for Christian beneficence, and 46 for good citizenship.

As each State was called out a delegate was sent forward. When all had assembled on the platform a hymn was sung and the delegates carried their pamphlets back to where their respective State delegations were seated.

The certificate is neatly arranged, contains the reasons why presented, and on the left side of the memorial is a banner with the words Christian Endeavor, inscribed in four different languages. The words on the certificate follow:

In witness of Notable Christian Service the United Society of Christian Endeavor gladly present this certificate to the Society of Christian Endeavor as a memorial of worthy effort along the lines indicated by a (*) during the year ended May 1, 1905:
*(1) *Devotional and Evangelistic Endeavor.* (2) *Committee Activities.* (3) *Educational Endeavor.* (4) *Christian Beneficence.* (5) *Good Citizenship Endeavor.*

Given at the Twenty-Second International Christian Endeavor Convention, Baltimore, July, 1905.

VON OGDEN VOGT,   FRANCIS E. CLARK,
General Secretary.   *President.*

PENNANT PRESENTATION

After the distribution of the pamphlets Dr. Hill announced the presentation of pennants and honorable mention for the following local unions for a gain in number of societies of at least 10 per cent.

Alabama — Birmingham and Jefferson county.
California — Alameda City and Ventura.
Connecticut — Norwich and Waterbury.
Illinois — McLean county, Rock Island county, Peoria district; South Division (Chicago), Q Division (Chicago), Hyde Park (Chicago).
Indiana — Indianapolis, Kokomo, Vincennes, Miami county, Muncie district, Crawfordsville district, and Indianapolis district.
Iowa — Fourth district.
Kentucky — Licking Valley and Louisville.
Louisiana — Southern district.
Maryland — Baltimore Juniors and Kent and Cecil counties.
Massachusetts — Fall River, Franklin county, Essex county, Lynn, Springfield, and Pittsfield.
Michigan — Saginaw, Lake Superior, Kalkaska, and Livingston counties.
Missouri — St. Louis, Central Division, St. Louis; and St. Joseph.
Minnesota — Tracy district, Windom and Duluth.
Nebraska — Omaha and Seventh district.
New Jersey — Hudson, Morris, and Sussex counties, Middlesex and Mizpah.
New York — Sixth, Third, and Fourth Divisions, New York; Seventh and First Divisions, Brooklyn; Otsego county, Tappan Zee, Allegany county, Buffalo Assembly, Utica, Lake Erie, Cortland county, Riga, Erie county, Binghamton, Troy Local, Troy district, Oneida county and Monroe county.
Ohio — Van Wert county, Seneca county, Miami county, Highland county, Cincinnati, Tiffin, Branch C (Cincinnati), Summit county, and Cleveland.
Pennsylvania — Center county, Berks county, Mifflin county, Bradford and Sullivan counties and Lycoming county.
Rhode Island — Washington county Central.
Tennessee — Memphis.
Vermont — Chittenden county, Caledonia county, Orleans county, Mizpah and Rutland counties.
Washington State — Seattle.
West Virginia — Clarksburg district.
Wisconsin — West Wisconsin district, South Central district.

CANADA

Manitoba — Winnipeg.
Quebec — Montreal.

As the States were called there were some unusual demonstrations. In every delegation by this time a banner or pennant of some kind had been erected, and as the name of each State was called out the whole delegation cheered, the pennant was waved, and the leader came forward and received the "recognition leaflets" to which his State was entitled from the secretary. Tremendous enthusiasm was created by the announcement that Ohio led every other State and country in the world in the gain made, as since November, 1902, 753 new societies had been added in that State. When this statement was made the Ohio delegation, seated near the stage in the center aisle, rose in a body and gave their State yell.

Ohio was cheered by the other delegates, and then Iowa began. With a tremendously enthusiastic delegation occupying a conspicuous place on the north side of the hall near the platform, they managed to center attention upon themselves by their volume and vehemence.

Gradually, when the applause had subsided, further announcements were made by Mr. Vogt, and the New York, Pennsylvania, West Virginia, Minnesota, Illinois, California and other delegations got an opportunity to greet the Convention with yells and salutations as they received their pennants and leaflets. One of the strongest was that of Pennsylvania, which had an immense delegation. There was something doing every minute, and the more enthusiastic the crowd grew the more Secretary Vogt and Treasurer Shaw smiled. At last Treasurer Shaw sprang up, and exclaimed: —

"I never attended a college commencement that I did not desire that I would some day see such enthusiasm displayed in a religious gathering. I have lived to see the college boy outdone. Shout out your yells. Lift up your voices. Let the world know that you believe in Christian Endeavor. I am glad that we can meet in this way, and I know you all feel just the same way."

STATES RECEIVE BANNERS

The great demonstration, however, came at the last, when Mr. Vogt made the presentation of the beautiful silken banners which were won by those States which have made a gain of 10 per cent, and more in their membership since November, 1902. The banners were of exquisite and beautiful workmanship and of many delicate shades and hues. Each, as it was raised on high and exhibited, brought forth shouts of acclaim and admiration. They had been specially ordered from Japan, China, Spain, and Mexico for this occasion, and the States to which they were given were: —

STATES.	Societies added since Nov. 1902.	Per cent of gain reported.
Arizona	7	20
Arkansas	72	33
California	173	$12\frac{1}{3}$
Hawaii Territory	25	116
Idaho	13	15
Kansas	175	$12\frac{1}{2}$
Iowa	208	12
Kentucky	61	$11\frac{1}{2}$
Michigan	166	10
Minnesota	123	13
Mississippi	16	$13\frac{1}{8}$
Montana	16	$19\frac{1}{2}$
New Jersey	171	$11\frac{1}{4}$
New York	45	$12\frac{1}{2}$
North Carolina	45	$10\frac{3}{4}$
Rhode Island	41	$13\frac{1}{2}$
South Carolina	26	$21\frac{1}{3}$
Tennessee	58	10
Texas	88	$10\frac{1}{2}$
Wyoming	7	$23\frac{1}{3}$
CANADA		
Alberta	5	$33\frac{1}{3}$
Manitoba	63	$36\frac{1}{2}$

Note. Many of the States had received their banners last year and so are not in the above list.

As the leading delegate from each of these States came forward to the speaker's platform to receive the banner, he or she turned to the great audience and expressed his or her sentiments. The general trend of the speeches was that the State which had won the banner was proud of what had been achieved, but that they intended to go back home with a renewed determination to surpass in the next two years the record made in the last two.

The California delegate declared that the banner was the only thing the Convention had yet given his State, but before long they would be assured that the next convention would meet in Los Angeles. This aroused the Kansas City delegation to an outburst of enthusiasm in behalf of their own city, which is making a strong fight for the next convention.

When the young lady from Minnesota had delivered her short address and started for her delegation with the banner held proudly over her head she was greeted with loud and prolonged yells from the delegation from her State, especially those from Minneapolis, which city is endeavoring to secure the next convention.

Kansas was presented with an imperial banner from China, on which was an enormous dragon. Dr. Hill facetiously remarked that the dragon was going to eat up Los Angeles, Seattle, and Minneapolis, and that the convention was going to Kansas City.

The banner presented to Kentucky was made in China and had inscribed upon it in Chinese the names of the Christian Endeavor martyrs who met death during the Boxer uprising, not many years ago.

Dr. F. D. Power, of Washington, then stepped forward and offered a prayer for the martyrs who had given their life for Christianity. The Convention, in a moment, underwent a remarkable transformation, and from the cheers and applause that reverberated throughout the vast auditorium there came silence, impressive and dignifying, and with heads bowed in solemn prayer the delegates listened to the affecting and sublime words uttered by Dr. Power.

Mr. Jacobs announced that he had to leave the city at noon, and that he would sing another solo for the Convention before departing. While silence reigned he sang in his rich and melodious voice a hymn that illustrated the purpose of the meeting, and the delegates joined in with him on the chorus.

Mr. Vogt then resumed the distribution of banners, but stated that there would be no more speeches from the delegates receiving the banners because too much time had already been consumed in the presentations. He simply called out the name of the State and handed the banner to the delegate who came forward to receive it. In concluding the distribution Mr. Vogt cited several States that were climbing up the ladder of gains very fast, and that they would add more stars to their banners when the next convention is held. He stated that Maryland had gained another 10 per cent since the last convention, and that she was now on her third 10 per cent.

He then asked the delegates from Oklahoma to stand up and hold aloft their banner. He called attention to the fact that the delegates had earned the right to place six stars on the banner for the excellent work they have accomplished, and, at this, the whole Convention arose to its feet and cheered the representatives from the Western State.

An Inspiring Scene

At this point the most inspiring and beautiful scene of the morning took place, when the delegates with their banners, numbering about fifty, paraded around the room. They lined up in front of the platform, and then marched in single file down the right side of the Armory, around the back of the hall and then up the left side to the platform, which they mounted and stretched out along its front, with their banners waving. The delegates on the floor, while the banners were being carried around the room, mounted to their chairs and gave cheer after cheer for the various States as they passed in review. While they were marching, the whole assemblage sang "Onward, Christian Soldiers," and the enthusiastic scene was indescribable, outdoing any previous Convention episode.

The speaker's platform was utilized by the delegates to display their flags, and they crowded onto chairs and tables. Kansas City and Los Angeles stood side by side, and in good-natured rivalry they piled chair upon chair in order to hold their banners, with the name of the State upon them, the highest in the air. The delegates then waved the banners back and forward in rhythmic motion, and then ensued the scene of the Convention. With the bright and varicolored banners as a background, and with the smiling countenances of the delegates on the floor looking at those on the platform, the assemblage broke forth into the exquisite strains of the national anthem, "Star-Spangled Banner," the whole audience standing. Each delegate waved his handkerchief at the banners on the stage as a salute, while they were singing the anthem. The banners were waved back and forth, and for a period of about five minutes the enthusiasm was great. With the cheers still reverberating throughout the hall, the delegates, bearing the banners, paraded around the hall again.

A noteworthy incident of this was that in the crowd while the singing was going on was a granddaughter of Francis Scott Key — Miss Alicia Key — who joined in the general enthusiasm awakened by the song of her illustrious ancestor.

Just before the meeting adjourned Secretary Vogt read the following telegram from Dr. Clark: —

> Express my deep interest in recognition service. Have been eagerly anticipating this service for months. Congratulate the successful Local Unions and States.

Three rousing cheers were given for Dr. Clark. If only he could have heard them by wireless telepathy!

CHAPTER XX

Christian Endeavor and Reforms

AT THE ARMORY, MONDAY AFTERNOON

Two noted public men were on the program for the afternoon, one of them not only a new member of President Roosevelt's cabinet, as Secretary of War, but also among the most honored citizens of Baltimore — honored because of his bold stand for political purity and his independence as a party man. Commissioner Henry B. F. Macfarland of the District of Columbia was equally worthy to represent Christian citizenship and civic reform. Besides, Rev. Mr. Stelzle was to speak for organized labor, and an English reformer, E. Tennyson Smith, for temperance. This was a field reform afternoon, and a program of unusual character.

As though the Convention must not close without recognizing the weather man once more as superlative, just before that session there set in another of those terrific downpours of rain that made travel difficult. Then, during the session, a thunderstorm broke, and Mr. Macfarland simply had to stop speaking while the congregation sang and sang again until the violence of the rain was over. From first almost to last, therefore, the struggle with the elements was continued. But the Convention beat. The victory was all on one side.

Secretary Vogt gathered what voice the morning had left him and presided at this session. Mr. Foster led the chorus. Mr. Stelzle made a strong plea for a different kind of treatment of the working men by the church. If it be true, he said, that the working men do not go to church, the church must go after them. If it is their fault, that is all the more reason for trying to get them to see their fault. That is the business of the church. This is the sound way he put it: —

> In our last presidential election the Socialists polled about six hundred thousand votes, a sevenfold increase since the preceding election. If the same ratio of increase continues, they will soon elect a president of the United States. But the phase of Socialism that is to be feared is that to many Socialism has become a substitute for the church. The church must recognize the element of truth there is in Socialism and must show the working man that it is offering him the same gospel it offers his employer.
>
> In the trades-unions of the country there are perhaps three million members, and the movement is growing in strength. The cure for bad unionsim is good unionism. If you drive the working men out of their labor organizations, you will drive them into Socialism.
>
> Socialism, communism, anarchism, are fundamentally moral problems. Be-

fore you can have an ideal society you must have ideal men, men who are controlled by Jesus Christ. Jesus Christ came to establish a kingdom of which He shall be the ruler and, when every knee shall bow and every tongue confess that Jesus Christ is Lord, then and only then shall the labor question be settled.

A great reception was accorded Hon. Charles J. Bonaparte, the chorus leading in the Chautauqua salute. He had a carefully prepared anti-political-corruption address, long and elaborate and worth reading thoughtfully. This was the line of his thought, his subject being "Politics and Religion": —

Many of our public questions, he said, are moral questions, but they are also religious questions because the religion of the Bible is primarily a moral religion, while mankind has known many religions that have been immoral. Politics with us implies some form of government by persuasion; without moral influence there would be room only for government by force.

The underlying evil in the administration of our public affairs is simply dishonesty. Our public offices are too often held by dishonest men, too often gained by dishonest means, too often used for dishonest ends. In law and morals alike a public office belongs to the people. Civil-service reform applies a caustic to the ulcer in our politics in the application of morality and common sense to the choice of public servants. To get rid of the typical politician we must eradicate the absurd notion that offices are spoils. This must be the first step if we would purify our politics. Pure politics means politics guided by sincere and unselfish men. Because we cannot expect a perfect government until the people that govern are also perfect the conclusion is not infrequently drawn that meantime any improvement is hopeless. But this is a grave mistake. No doubt there never will be a perfect government of men by men, but there are forms much better than those we now live under. The question of good government in America is essentially a moral, and only incidentally a political one.

Alexander Hamilton was not much more of a saint than the man who killed him, but there was between them just the difference which made for the men of their day and makes for history all the difference possible. When, therefore, we speak of "pure politics," we mean politics guided and controlled by sincere, scrupulous, and unselfish men. The politics of any community can be "purified" only by leading such men to engage in them and driving other men out of them; and each of us aids in the "purifying" process when he tries to render a political career attractive to our best citizens, and does what he can to make the worst gain a living otherwise.

If we wait for existing evils to be cured by some great change to come somehow, and while it is coming content ourselves with telling what we will do when it comes, it will not come at all; but if, dealing with a present duty, we obey the voice of honor and conscience, and do what we know ought to be done now and here, that which we dream probably will come to pass. As we strive to gain a better government, we shall deserve one; and, as we deserve this, we shall have it. Freedom is not the birthright of slumberers.

"Those serve truth best who to themselves are true,
And what they dare to dream of dare to do."

Mr. E. Tennyson Smith, of Birmingham, England, the well-known temperance advocate, on being introduced to speak on the progress in temperance reform, referred to the freedom of English audiences in expressing their approval or disapproval of the speaker's utterances, and wished his hearers to be as free. "I believe," said he, "that all progress in temperance reform must come from the Christian church. You will understand, therefore, that I expect much from the Christian Endeavor movement. I take my stand on God's word; and, if there is not teetotalism and prohibition in this book, I will have none of them.

"I take my stand on this verse: 'For this purpose was the Son of God manifested, that he might destroy the works of the devil.' I ask you, Is the liquor traffic the work of the devil?" "Yes," came the response from the audience. "What are you going to do? The church of God is intended to carry out Christ's purpose, is it not? Say 'Yes' or 'No.'" "Yes," came again the decided answer. "Then it is the church's business to destroy the liquor traffic."

The liquor traffic, he said in impassioned tones, was the most gigantic machinery this side of the lower regions in the service of the devil. He said that a million persons die every year as a result of the drink habit. "But figures mean nothing and convey no idea of the suffering," he said. Then he suddenly brought into view a huge black roll. He tossed one end of it on the edge of the platform, and it fell to the floor and rolled along the hall. "This," he said, holding up his end of the roll, "is made of clippings taken from papers published in England for the week before Christmas, 1903, and the first week in January, 1904. The roll is thirty-six yards long and the clippings came from our English newspapers — mind you, not your American ones — and they show a total of 3,290 crimes, murders, suicides, caused in those two weeks by the drink." He referred to the subway tavern in New York by saying, "It is the duty of the Christian church to destroy this liquor traffic — not to blaspheme God by going to New York and opening a saloon with singing the Doxology.

The Christian man who lets his premises to a saloon he classed as a Christian humbug, and he condemned scathingly the church that accepts money from liquor sellers.

He intimated that he had heard during his stay in this country that its politics was extremely corrupt. "Is politics a muddy pool in America? Then you Christian men go into the pool and cleanse it."

"I want a message from you to England. Every Christian Endeavorer ought as a Christian to be a total abstainer. Is that right?" "Yes," came in no uncertain tones from the thousands of voices. "It is the duty of every Christian Endeavorer to be determined to destroy the liquor traffic. Is that so?" "Yes," once more.

"I know we are going to win in this temperance question. Why? The liquor traffic rules in England, and it rules in America. But there is something higher than the British government, something higher than the American government; the government is upon His shoulder.

> "'Jesus shall reign where'er the sun
> Does his successive journeys run,
> His kingdom stretch from shore to shore
> Till moons shall wax and wane no more.'"

"A high type of Christian citizen" was Secretary Vogt's way of introducing Commissioner Macfarland, who was to speak on "Responsibility for Public Opinion." He was given a vigorous Chautauqua salute. In presenting the greetings of the capital city he referred to the recollections of Washington, 1896, expressed pleasure at the prospect of the Christian Endeavor memorial building, and suggested that it be located at Washington.

Public opinion, he said, governs everywhere. Wherever there is self-government, responsibility for public opinion is shared by all. Voting is confined to a minority, and is cumbersome and uncertain, but public opinion is as efficient and instantaneous as a stroke of lightning. We who believe that all of the people are wiser than any of the people must see that the most perfect system is that where public opinion is most enlightened.

The audience in the vast Armory knew how to appreciate a voice that could be easily heard, and Mr. Macfarland had uttered but two words when they burst into applause. But another of the heavy showers of the Convention week had come up while he was speaking, and the roar of the rain on the roof drowned out even his strong tones, and he was forced to wait. Nothing but Christian Endeavor singing could make itself heard, and "Coronation," "Blest be the tie," "America," and "Alas, and did my Saviour bleed?" followed one after the other.

Resuming, Mr. Macfarland said the speech was the most restful he had ever delivered, and he wished he might always have Mr. Foster and the audience at hand ready to sing in the middle of his speeches, which would then be much more effective. This graceful turn brought down the house.

We must give place to this fine passage, which sets forth Christian Citizenship most forcibly and finely and should be quoted everywhere: —

It must be evident that no duty of the citizen is more important than that which is the duty of all citizens, — the forming and the exerting of public opinion. It is our duty to make honest return of our property and to pay our taxes. It is our duty, if we are men, to serve on the jury and in the militia (and not to serve on one for the sake of escaping the claims of the other) or to respond to the government's call to face mobs of rioters or lynchers, just as it is our duty, whether we hold office or not — and some of us must serve the State by holding office, even at a sacrifice — to support, defend, and obey the Constitution and the laws. It is the duty of the limited number who have the right of suffrage to exercise it, not superstitiously as though it had any virtue or value in itself, but as the only official method of expressing public opinion. But, above all these duties, the good citizen of either sex, of any age, will hold supreme in its privilege and its responsibility the duty of governing by public opinion. How is that high office to be executed?

First — Assuming always that the citizen so lives as to have the respect and regard of fellow-citizens, since otherwise he has no influence with them. Let him inform himself carefully about the men and the acts, the principles and the propositions upon which he must pass; hear both sides before deciding. Let no one have to ask you to suspend judgment until you get all the facts that can be had. There is a popular tyranny worse than that of any despot, and its most cruel expression is in hasty judgments on half the facts.

Second — Having reached a conclusion after careful examination and deliberation, express it in conversation, in letters to the newspapers and to public men, and, if necessary, in public meetings which you may help to organize. Thus you will inform and influence public opinion, drawing together all those of like mind and purpose, and if you really have a good cause it must prevail sooner or later. Even bad causes prevail, at least temporarily, when their agents are skilful in influencing public opinion, and you may rest assured that they never neglect their work in this respect, even if the good citizens do neglect their duty. But we who believe that God rules in the affairs of nations cannot doubt that what is right must win in the long run.

Now, all the other duties of a citizen are light and easy compared with this one. And it is constant, while they are infrequent. Moreover, there is little prospect of any other return than the success of the effort. The good citizen, however, will not be deterred by the difficulties; he will rather welcome them. And he is not working for personal reward, like those traitors to the State who take bribes in any form for their votes.

This was truly a Christian Citizenship session, and worthy to rank in importance with any that had preceded. What a variety, and each fitting perfectly in its place. This one made for the righteousness that exalteth a nation.

Stephen Jones

Miss Ellen M. Stone

Rev. William E. Biederwolf, D.D.

Bishop Arnett

Rev. Luther de Yoe

Bishop Alexander Walters

CHAPTER XXI

The Closing Session

AT THE ARMORY, MONDAY EVENING

The President's Address and Roll Call of States

THE supreme hour of a superlative Convention! Again the great host, apparently unwearied. Again the scenes of unbounded enthusiasm, although wholly different from those of the morning. For the last time the outbreaking applause as, after the thousands were in place, the vast space was suddenly darkened, and then one by one shone out the shields and badge and monogram and legend which had each evening delighted the audience. Somehow this time the motto, "The World for Christ" seemed to take on new significance, as the accumulated interest and spiritual and evangelistic influence of the week pressed upon the mind and heart. "It is good to be here" was the universal feeling, as though a new mount of vision had been reached, whence could be seen the army of Christ advancing to mighty victories for peace and truth and righteousness.

It was fitting that at this session Treasurer Shaw should again preside. He is Dr. Clark's longest and closest associate in the great work. Most fitting it was also that Mr. John Willis Baer, so long the beloved general secretary of the United Society and known to Endeavorers in all parts of the world, should be present to read the Annual Message of the absent president to the young people. Mr. Baer is now one of the secretaries of the Presbyterian Home Mission Board, doing an important work for America; he is also secretary of the World's Christian Endeavor Union. So everything was in the best possible shape for this closing session, seeing that the president could not be on hand to inspire, as he peculiarly knows how to, in the last hours of a convention. No man has the quiet power of Dr. Clark in drawing out others and impelling them to renewed consecration. This was always his favorite session. A mighty Convention without him, the leader, what would it have been with him!

But it was a Clark meeting from beginning to end — one that would have greatly embarrassed him could he have been concealed behind a pillar and seen and heard the demonstrations of affection and the words of praise and love.

The Opening Scenes

The enthusiasm of this crowning session of a singularly splendid series was contagious. It was in the atmosphere. The afternoon shower had been the clearing one, and there was a freshness in the air not felt before. At last the elements smiled. So the Endeavor enthusiasm began to manifest itself with the arrival of the State delegations, each singing its own favorite hymn, and gained momentum until the time for calling the State roll, when the wave of feeling, like some visible, tangible thing, gained the upper hand and took hold of the 15,000 in ocean-like billows that surged from end to end and from roof to floor of the Armory, sweeping everybody with it.

First came a song service. Led by Mr. Foster, the vast audience and chorus united their voices in flooding the hall with "Onward Christian Soldiers" and "Forward." "It sounds better every time we sing it; now let's sing another verse," said Mr. Foster many times over, and as many times did the host respond, louder and more enthusiastically at each singing.

"The next hymn is 'All Hail the Power of Jesus' Name,'" said Mr. Foster, and the singers responded as one tremendous multiple voice, overwhelmed with religious fervor.

Then Mr. Hatch led in prayer. "Fulfil the promise of Thy Holy Spirit, that this may be not only the best session of this Convention, but the best session of all our conventions."

The chorus sung Gounod's "Send out Thy light," — and how gloriously they sung it! They made that the keynote of the evening and of the Convention. Could that chorus know all the good its singing did, the members would feel fully compensated for all their time and sacrifice.

Mr. Shaw announced a special message from Dr. Clark, and Secretary Vogt read it, as follows: —

With all my heart I wish to thank my kind friends who, by letter and telegrams from Baltimore and from many parts of the country, have sent me so many cordial and affectionate messages of sympathy and good will. I cannot reply to all individually and so I crave a moment of time at the closing session of the Convention and will ask our secretary to express my gratitude to all.

"Also I am most thankful for the generous resolutions that have reached me from the Convention and from State delegations, and appreciate more than I can tell the many assurances of hearty support for the cause we all hold dear. All these kind expressions and these promises of earnest prayer have given me new courage and cheer and have only strengthened my desire to give myself more unreservedly in the future to the cause of Christ, the church, and the young people.

"I rejoice in the splendid Convention, of which I have had so many assurances by letter and through the press; and believe that God has the best things yet in store for us in this new quarter of a century of Christian Endeavor which we shall so soon begin. I am, gratefully and fraternally yours,

Francis E. Clark.

A tender and touching prayer was then offered by Vice-President Grose for the speedy recovery of Dr. Clark. "Even while we unitedly pray, let the life-giving breezes of the sea blow upon him in his far cottage on the Maine shore, and let this hour be the beginning of new strength, that his precious life may be spared long years to come to the cause he loves and for which he has given his life." All joined in that heartfelt plea.

"I surrender all" was sung exquisitely by the choir, the host joining in the chorus, and the audience was ready for the message of the founder.

"We are going to be just as enthusiastic to-night as any night before this one," said Mr. Shaw, before the reading of the message. "This closing service has already been more enthusiastic than any other, if that be possible, but we are going to show our enthusiasm in a different way. When the roll of States is called you will give your selected songs, but the State yells will be omitted. And before Dr. Clark's address is read the delegations will turn down their State signs.

"Our motto shall be 'Send out the light.' I hold in my hand an old shoemaker's hammer used by the original William Carey, the father of modern missions, who cobbled shoes in England more than a century ago. In the inspiration of this old hammer let us go from this meeting determined to send forth the light. I must turn to the chorus and tell them that the good accomplished by these meetings is largely due to their efforts and that their songs have helped us in feeling the need of sending out the light." The chorus waved handkerchiefs in appreciation.

"At no time during these meetings have we missed the presence of our beloved Dr. Clark as we do to-night. Let us listen to his address in perfect quiet."

He then introduced, as the reader, one who had worked with Dr. Clark for twelve years in closest intimacy, one who loved and knew him as few did. As Mr. Baer took the speaker's stand, the whole audience rose, gave him the Chautauqua salute, then great applause broke forth. It was a greeting of genuine delight, and he was deeply affected. He expressed his joy at standing before a Christian Endeavor audience once more, and such an audience as this! Dr. Clark's regretted illness had given him this great privilege. He paid noble tribute to the disinterestedness and self-sacrifice of Dr. Clark's work, then proceeded to the business in hand, to make effective the leader's message. Amid closest attention he read, as follows: —

THE EVANGELIZATION OF OUR YOUNG PEOPLE, OUR
COUNTRY, AND THE WORLD

A Program for Beginning the Twenty-fifth Year of Christian Endeavor

The occasion gives us our theme to-day. Christian Endeavor is approaching its first great annniversary. In a few months more a full quarter of a century will have been completed since the first society was established and the modern young people's movement was begun. From this high vantage-ground we do well to look both ways, backward for encouragement, forward with hope and new aspirations.

We need dwell upon the past only long enough to gain courage for the future. Within the compass of these years the movement has grown from one society to more than 66,000; from less than fifty members to nearly 4,000,000, besides many millions more who have graduated into other lines of church work. It has found its way into every part of the world, and has its home practically in every nation. It is established now in sixty different nations and colonies, among peoples who speak nearly one hundred different languages and dialects, into which its constitution and some portions of its literature have been translated. Its weekly or monthly publications are found in almost every civilized country and tongue.

The Roster of Christian Endeavor

When we call the roll of our brotherhood, Great Britain responds with nearly 10,000 societies, Canada and Australia with thousands more, India with more than 600, China with 300 societies, and Japan with half as many more. Germany's strong contingent is ever increasing, as is that of almost every European country, while Africa and the islands of the sea add many thousands of Endeavorers to our fellowship.

Since last we met in International Convention I have seen our comrades in New Zealand, Tasmania, and all the states of the Australian Commonwealth, in South Africa, in England, Ireland, Scotland, and Wales, and several European countries, and can testify to the vigor and growing power of Christian Endeavor in all these lands.

When we come nearer home, we find that America's tens of thousands of societies have had a period of great activity since last the reckoning was made, as our secretary's most heartening report has shown. The Increase Campaign has resulted in a great gain in numbers and, I believe, in spiritual activities as well.

Such a history, though recounted ever so briefly, must increase the humility as well as the gratitude of every Endeavorer, as he remembers that these results could not be of man, or the power of man, but of God. We will dwell upon them only long enough to get a new impetus for the future.

For nearly twenty-five years we have been steadily climbing the hills of Christian Endeavor progress. Each year has seen some advance upon the last in numbers, activities, and spiritual attainments. And now we have come to this coign of vantage of a twenty-five years' retrospect. But, as when in climbing the Alps, mountains seem to rise on mountains, and there are ever new peaks to scale, so this summit on which we stand only reveals new heights which we have yet to climb. We could not see them from below; for the nearer mountains, not yet surmounted, hid them from our view. But now that we have nearly reached this quarter-century peak, we see them still looming beyond us.

Let me, then, suggest some higher summits of achievement, or at least of endeavor, which I see before us, as we follow the same upward path. These endeavors are all in the line of the evangelistic spirit, which have been the keynote of this Convention, and which will, I profoundly believe, be the keynote of the church of the twentieth century.

A Revival Century

We are living in years of revival interest, thank God. As the historian a hundred years hence looks back to the earlier years of this twentieth century, he will describe it as a decade of revival, a revival of interest in spiritual things, a revival of missionary zeal, a revival of civic and corporate righteousness.

The evangelist is coming to his own again. Materialism has had its day for the present; and spiritual truth is taking its place as the only reality.

Then, fellow Endeavorers, let us put ourselves in the way of God's plans; let us allow Him to use us in the great revival which is on the way, which is even now with us, though perhaps we know it not. And let us take for our high aim and purpose nothing less than *the evangelization of our young people, our country, and the world.*

Such a theme is but the continuation of the history of the past quarter of a century, an advance step in the line of march God has marked out for Christian

Endeavor. May we not humbly claim that He has been preparing the way for the present world-wide revival in part by these twenty-five years of Christian Endeavor work, and that he has equipped and girded us, as He did Cyrus of old, for this supreme hour? The history of Christian Endeavor has been the history of successive revivals. It was born in a spiritual awakening, and its years of growth have been marked by the revival of the prayer-meeting, the revival of practical service by the young people through their committees, the revival of missionary zeal and giving, the revival of good citizenship, the revival of personal communion with God through the Quiet Hour, the revival of interdenominational, international fellowship among young Christians. Is not the time ripe, I say, for a new, united, persistent, untiring effort for this all-comprehensive revival, *the evangelization of our young people, our country, and the world?*

A GREAT PROGRAM

Does this seem to be a purpose too large and ambitious for a society composed chiefly of young people? But it cannot be too large, if it is Christ's purpose for us. He would have us adopt a program no smaller or less comprehensive, and in His great program we can each have our little part.

How can it be done? Not in a day or a year; but by persistence, faith, patience, laboring together with God and with one another, all things are possible.

By every enlargement and improvement of our societies we are so far forth evangelizing the young people. By helping in every way our own churches and mission boards we are evangelizing our country and the world.

Let me, then, mention four special lines of effort which are appropriate to every society, by which we may signalize the beginning of our second quarter-century. Many can undertake other things; these are within the range of all, the smallest and the largest, in country and city alike.

I. An endeavor for larger societies.
II. An endeavor for a revival of church-going.
III. An endeavor for an increase of church-membership.
IV. An endeavor for a revival of missionary zeal and giving.

First. In our evangelistic effort, let us begin at our own Jerusalem, building each over against his own house. Let us seek earnestly for more active and associate and affiliated members, for until we draw the young people into some relation with our work we cannot hope to help them. Many societies ought to double and treble their numbers within a twelvemonth. Their first duty is to reach out after all the young men and women and boys and girls in their church circle, and bring them, if possible, into some relation with the society as the center of the religious life for the young. Our Increase Campaign has been largely directed to the formation of new societies. Let us widen its scope so as to include a strenuous effort for the enlargement of old societies. This is a practical, definite, evangelistic service that may well engage the attention of every society and every union.

AN ENDEAVOR TO PROMOTE CHURCH-GOING

Second. But Christian Endeavor is never satisfied with simply building up its own ranks. It exists for Christ and the church and the world. Then let us mark our anniversary by a renewed effort to bring others into the church and into its membership. We are told that in many places the habit of church-going has for years been gradually waning. Why should not Endeavorers seek more earnestly to correct this tendency, and to promote among their companions love and reverence for the house of God? I allude not only to the Sunday morning and evening services, but to the weekly prayer-meeting of the church, and the Sunday school. Let us from this time make it one of our chief aims to induce our friends and comrades to come into the house of God, believing that there the sweet influence of its worship and aspiration, of Scripture and prayer and praise, may create within them a love of these heavenly things. The revivals of old frequently began in a new regard for the house of God. So it was in the time of Ezra and Nehemiah, of Hezekiah and Josiah. Let Christian Endeavor say practically to all the world, like the prophet of old, "Come ye, and let us go up to the house of God; and he will teach us of his ways, and we will walk in his paths."

Third. Again, let us strive for a great increase of church-membership. Our associate members give us our field and our evangelistic opportunity. Literally millions of them during the past twenty-five years have come to Christ and into the churches of all denominations. But other millions should come. No society is doing its whole duty that is not a stepping-stone to full membership in the church of Christ. From the Junior society are more and more recruits coming into the church, and yet there are multitudes of children, whose tender hearts are most easily touched by the story of the cross, who have not yet taken this step. It presupposes conversion, of course, and thus makes of our societies, if we set this before us as one of our chief aims, a great evangelistic agency. Such a revival will vastly enlarge the churches, strengthen the cause of Christ on earth, and cause joy in the presence of the angels of God.

To Save Our Country and the World

Fourth. Another revival effort that is within the scope of every society, large or small, is that of increased missionary effort, especially in the raising of money for the spread of the kingdom of God in our own and every land. This, too, has long been an endeavor of Endeavorers; but there are heights of self-sacrifice and generous giving for the spread of the Kingdom which we must yet scale if we would be true to our great commission. I plead with you to forget the things which are behind, and to reach forward to the larger and more generous things that are before.

The salvation of our own country from the forces of greed and corruption and ring rule and rum rule, the good-citizenship plank of our Christian Endeavor platform, is closely allied with home missions, which in short means nothing less than the redemption of all America. Thus Patriotism adds its voice to Religion in urging us to pray and work and give for the evangelization of these great States and Provinces.

No society lives up to the principles of Christian Endeavor which does not make at least some contribution, large or small, according to its ability, to both the home and the foreign work of its own denomination. While we are catholic in our views and generous in our efforts for all the needy, let us remember that our first duty is to give in and through our own churches for the support of the missionary enterprises that are especially committed to them. Study the situation; give not only generously, but wisely, considering carefully what proportion of the money that you can give shall go to your own missionary board, what to your own church, and what to special causes that strongly appeal to you and which you should also help.

An Endeavor for Millions

Before I close I would, if possible, set before you some more definite and tangible goals. Christian Endeavor is nothing if not practical. It does not deal in glittering generalities, but seeks for actual results. So, in order to attain the objects I have suggested, let us set before ourselves these great *definite* aims as we look forward to the beginning of a new and larger era:

A million new members brought into our societies.

A million people brought to church, or prayer-meeting, or Sunday school.

A million young people brought into membership in the church of the living God.

A million dollars for missions at home and abroad, given through our denominational boards.

Here are four large, practical, definite, attainable endeavors, four efforts which will greatly promote the interest of the church throughout the world, four things which He would like to have us do.

Many denominations and organizations wisely utilize their great anniversaries by raising large funds for their important enterprises. Let us signalize the twenty-fifth year of the modern young people's movement by beginning a campaign, not only for dollars, but for millions of young men and women, and boys and girls. Let me repeat:

A MILLION NEW CHRISTIAN ENDEAVORERS.
A MILLION NEW CHURCH-GOERS.
A MILLION NEW CHURCH-MEMBERS.
A MILLION NEW DOLLARS FOR DENOMINATIONAL MISSIONS.

Do you say that these are large figures, that many societies are small and weak, in scattered communities, with few people to influence, and little money? I can only reply that we ought to strive for large things, for we are laborers together with Him, and that, if each one does his little best, the aggregate will soon mount up into the millions.

Remember once more for our encouragement the record of the past. Over and over again has God surprised us, and rebuked our little faith by giving us more than we expected. When the Increase Campaign began, less than three years ago, it seemed impossible that in so short a time many of our States should add ten, twenty, or thirty per cent to their number. But thousands of new societies have been the result, and the campaign is still going on with undiminished force. It has spread into every land, and Great Britain as well as America, Asia and Africa as well as Europe, have their Increase Campaigns, which are rapidly multiplying the number of our comrades and the value of their work; so why should we not expect, and within a reasonable time, too, to reach our million goals? Let us each contribute our small quota, and the work is done.

A SUGGESTED MOTTO

In the past years you have more than once allowed me to suggest a motto, which you have generously adopted as your own. Here is one which I ask you to take for this year as a source of inspiration and encouragement. It was given us first by that old warrior apostle Paul, who was always endeavoring, always achieving, always leaving past attainments behind, always pressing forward to new heights. For our twenty-fifth anniversary year he seems to have written these inspiring words:

"*In one spirit, with one mind, striving together for the faith of the gospel.*"

How exactly appropriate to Christian Endeavor! "I will strive to do whatever He would like to have me do," we have all said a hundred times. The best translation of "endeavor" in many languages is "striving together." "Striving together" in Europe and Asia and Africa and America. "Striving together" in every continent and all the islands of the sea. "Striving together" for these millions which will mean so much for the advancement of the kingdom. "Striving *together*," Baptists and Methodists, Presbyterians and Disciples of Christ, Congregationalists and Lutherans and Episcopalians, but all striving for the faith of the gospel. "Striving together" to bring men to the sanctuary; "striving together" to bring men to Christ and into His church; "striving together" to raise money by which the gospel can be sent to the remotest part of our own and other lands; "striving together," though far apart; striving in our prayer-meetings, our committees, our unions, and our great conventions; always "*in one spirit, with one mind, striving together for the faith of the gospel.*"

In the reading Mr. Baer emphasized various points. After the introductory summary of the growth of Christian Endeavor and its wide spread throughout the world, at Mr. Baer's suggestion the vast audience rose and sung with mighty melody the long-meter doxology. In connection with the plea of our president for a spirit of evangelism,

Mr. Baer reminded us that the Society was founded in a revival, and has maintained the revival spirit through all these years. The plea for a million dollars for our denominational mission boards during the coming year was received by the Endeavorers with tremendous applause, as were the other practical, definite suggestions, for a million new members in our societies, a million new church-goers, a million new church-members. All hearts went out to accept the motto which Dr. Clark suggested for our new year's work: "In one spirit, with one mind, striving together for the faith of the gospel." The hearty spirit showed the unanimous approval of the ringing call to large things.

Then Mr. Shaw took the stand, and introduced some features not on the program. "Have you ever known such a Convention as this?" he shouted. "No!" was thundered back at him. "This Convention to me is the Superlative Convention. [Great applause.] Baltimore, '05, has been great in everything." [More applause.] The leader was now in his irrepressible vein, and the audience rose to it. One of the great scenes was on. Every sentiment was greeted with laughter and applause, the chorus often leading.

"If I climbed to the topmost point in this immense Armory, and if my voice could go as high, I could not do justice to this wonderful Convention. Have you ever heard of a Convention like this! Every convention is known by a name, and I think the only fitting name for this is the 'Superlative Convention.'

"It has been great in everything. I never saw rain that was wetter, nor heat that was hotter; even the thunder is muffled by your applause, and the lightning is dimmed by the brilliance of these meetings.

"Think of it! Here is a hall one third larger than any other hall or tent in which a convention was ever held. Think of the crowds that have been here and the enthusiasm that has been expressed. Not momentary enthusiasm, but one week of solid, continued, growing enthusiasm. Oh, it is a great Convention. And think of those responsible for it. Thank the Committee of 1905. They are the people who ran the machinery without a jar."

When the Committee of 1905 was mentioned a white sea of fifteen thousand handkerchiefs waved joyfully for a prolonged minute. The speaker was compelled to stop his speech and wait until the enthusiasm quieted.

"Now, I want to introduce that Committee," he said, and was again drowned with cheers and waving of handkerchiefs. While the cheering was going on he took Chairman Atwood by the hand and led him to the platform, which proved a signal for another billow of enthusiasm. Then with a wave of his hand the entire Committee walked to the platform, and the enthusiasm surged in another great wave.

"This Committee is composed of all good men," he said. "We may say they mutually excel each other. This is the chairman, Mr. Atwood; he will tell you about the rest."

Several moments elapsed before Mr. Atwood could begin. Each

time that he tried another burst of cheering or handclapping delayed him. He had little to say, however, and smilingly waited till the ovation in his honor had subsided. "The success of this Convention," he said, "was not due to the work of the committees, but by God's grace to the zeal and enthusiasm of the people here assembled."

In words of highest praise he spoke of the work of the sub-committees and the scores who contributed their part toward the achievement. To these obscure workers, he said, is due much credit. The success of the Convention, he declared, was so great that all who had contributed anything toward it should feel amply repaid and fully convinced that his or her labors had reaped full fruit.

He then introduced the members of the Committee of 1905. Each name was greeted with applause, and many of the more popular committee-men were called upon for a speech, but the time would not allow the wish to be gratified.

Then the musical directors were called for and an ovation greeted Mr. Harris, Mr. Bonner, and Mr. Foster. Mr. Jacobs had gone home. One of the prettiest of the impromptu incidents now occurred, due to Mr. Foster's quick wit. It was not the intention of Mr. Foster and Mr. Bonner to come forward, but at an unexpected moment there arose a demand from the vast audience which could not be withstood. Then at the suggestion of Mr. Foster the incident was contrived which was one of the happiest of the Convention. Led by Mr. Bonner, who is from London, the great Convention chorus and the audience sang the national hymn of Great Britain, "God save the King." Led by Mr. Foster, they sang "My Country, 'tis of Thee." Following this and amid the most intense enthusiasm the two leaders, one of Washington and the other of London, together led the assemblage in the hymn "Blest be the tie that binds."

At the conclusion of the hymn continuous and prolonged applause seemed to flood the Armory like a tidal wave. Some one called for the brilliant but modest organist, and the applause continued until at length he rose and bowed. It was hard to settle down after this overflow.

At this happy time Dr. Hill was introduced to read the elaborate resolutions and restatement of Endeavor principles, the points of which were heartily received.

THE RESOLUTIONS

Gathered in the Twenty-second International Convention we recognize the favoring Providence that brought us to the Monumental City under circumstances so plainly propitious, and desire publicly to voice our thanks to Almighty God that our willing feet were turned hitherward, with so happy and fruitful and beneficent a result.

If we should fail to respond to the unbounded and unfailing kindnesses and courtesies of the people of Baltimore the stone would cry out of the wall and the beam out of the timber would answer it. The hospitality has seemed to us instinctive, truly and nobly Southern, and its inimitable method and charm have increased its welcome. With warm and full hearts we thank his Excellency the Governor, his Honor the Mayor, the ministers and officiary of the local churches, the busy pastors of this great community, the noble committee, by whose personnel and spirit and outstanding ability we have been so much impressed, without whose conspicuous success our Convention could not have been in our history what it has become. Our gratitude extends to 600 ushers, to 1,600 workers, to the senior and junior choirs of 2,400 voices, to the city authorities for generous appropriations, for splendid illuminations; to the board of trustees of the Fifth Regiment Armory, who have given us this spacious edifice freely; to the regimental companies, who simply vacated their twenty-five rooms and placed them gratuitously at our disposal: to the newspapers of Baltimore, not only for all they have done, but for the sympathy and the method with which they have done most acceptable work.

We congratulate the city upon having risen so speedily, phœnix-like, unaided, from the ashes of its terrible ordeal, its affliction by fire, and upon its full ability so soon to entertain so large a company of young people, who have assembled and carried on their work with an enthusiasm that the fire could not devour nor the floods of the last week drown.

The evangelistic meeting of last Sunday afternoon stands in our history unapproached. All the features give us what we are forced to style the superlative Convention.

We desire to put on record our expression of our respect for every man's faith, be he Jew or Catholic. We believe it an inalienable right to worship God according to the dictates of one's own conscience, and any leaflets distributed here that were offensive to such people as have been named were given out without our knowledge or consent. We repudiate the offensive leaflets and we apologize for them. We ask to be adjudged by our acts and not by the conduct of hangers-on about the Armory doors.

We stand for temperance; we believe in abstinence from intoxicants; we are clear that God-hated drunkeries are a peril to boys and young men. We commit ourselves to good citizenship and strive to see public problems from the standpoint of the home, in whose purity and integrity we believe, menaced, as it is to-day in one part of the West, by a relic of sheer barbarism and generally imperiled by the disgraceful extent of the divorce evil, exaggerated by the public calamity of a non-national divorce law. We stand for an evangelistic type of our holy religion, for the redemptive features of the doctrines of grace, and, as the churches are now shaping themselves for normal evangelism, we keep in line with the churches' movement toward revivals and the religious uses of Sunday nights. When the church plans new work on evangelistic lines we want to be a medium and an agency ready made to hand for the church's use.

It is our resolve to key our work, as this Convention has been attuned, to the evangelistic note; we stand for the Sabbath and congratulate Baltimore and Maryland on the excellence of their Sabbath laws here sustained; we stand for religious devotion, the covenant pledge, attendance on our services and participation in them for denominational loyalty and for interdenominational fellowship. We subordinate our young people to the pastor and to the officers of the local church, and no one utterance has ever issued from us that is not consonant with this fact. We are not separate from the church, but in the church and of the church and for the church, being under control of the local church Christian young people, helping young people. We are out and out for missions with their two correllates — on the one hand mission-study classes and on the other hand systematic proportionate giving.

We heartily indorse the project of gathering on the occasion of our twenty-fifth anniversary a memorial fund honoring the founder of these societies, likewise strengthening and extending our work; the money to be in part raised by a gift from all past and present members, of one cent each for each year of our radiant history.

Christian Endeavor Principles Restated

Gathered in the Twenty-second International Convention on our twenty-fourth anniversary, we note, with a new joy the effective uses of the principles that have made us great and made us grow. In November, 1902, it was proposed that we begin an increase, or forward, a betterment, campaign. It has succeeded beyond the anticipations of the most sanguine, resulting in specific forms of fruitfulness already reported from 5,422 distinct societies.

May we not now ask to be judged by our fruits, and may not we seek for unity on the basis of a liberal interpretation of the principles for which we are known to stand.

As societies are formed under varying conditions in great cities on the one hand, and in scattered communities on the other, on mission fields, and in halls of learning, and as it is a primary principle with us that we recognize the pastor in authority over his own young people, taking the initiative in their forms of service, the United Society does not insist upon uniform conditions of organization or a particular form of pledge which shall constitute a Christian Endeavor Society.

"So long as a society, holding the fundamental principles of Christian Endeavor, is working for Christ and the church as its church directs, and is making the young people 'more useful in the service of God,' it is in fact a society of Christian Endeavor and will be heartily welcomed into the fellowship of the movement."

The fundamental principles of the Society of Christian Endeavor are the following: —

First. Personal and avowed devotion to our divine Lord and Saviour Jesus Christ.

Second. The covenant obligation as particularly embodied in a pledge or covenant to do what Christ would like to have us do.

Third. Constant religious training for all kinds of Christian service in the prayer-meeting and by various committees.

Fourth. Loyalty to the local church and denomination with which each society is connected.

Fifth. Interdenominational spiritual fellowship; through which we hope to fulfil our Lord's prayer, for spiritual unity, "that they all may be one."

Sixth. Christian Endeavor makes no attempt, and never has attempted, to legislate for the individual conscience, and neither the United Society nor any state or local union regulates, controls or imposes conditions upon any society of Christian Endeavor.

These unions are for fellowship, instruction, and inspiration and not for legislation or for the exercise of control. If any society is in doubt as to methods of organization or service, it should turn for authoritative instruction to the pastor and church with which it is connected.

Relation of Christian Endeavor to Students in Colleges and Seminaries

Resolved That we view with solicitude the fact that the thousands of our young men and women, who are in college during four years when they naturally would be engaged in young people's work in the local home church, are thus to a large extent deprived of the inspiration and training of Christian Endeavor. Instead of returning to their churches with intelligent enthusiasm for the work their church is doing through its society, they in too many cases are indifferent to their duty and their opportunity in this work. The young men who continue their studies in the theological seminaries too seldom find that preparation for this work which its importance to the minister demands.

We covet these splendid young people in college, university, and seminary for the work in the church for which this organization stands, and it is our conviction that our Society should no longer refrain from facing its duty toward them for their own sakes and for the sake of the young people of the churches where they are so soon to take their place of leadership.

After the audience had unanimously and heartily adopted the resolutions and statement, Dr. Hill proved at once his faith in the testimonial movement in most practical manner by suggesting gifts to it in honor of departed Endeavorers, and to show what he meant, he himself subscribed twenty-five dollars each, in honor of William H. Pennell, the first president of the United Society of Christian Endeavor; Choate Burnham, a stanch friend of the cause in its early days; Clarence E. Eberman, our lamented field secretary; Willis Baer, the little son whom Secretary Baer lost; and John Manning Barrows, the son of John Henry Barrows, who had written to Dr. Hill that his most precious memory connected with his son was that he had testified for Christ in a Christian Endeavor meeting the Sunday before his death. This was another of the unexpected but gracious things, and was heartily applauded.

The Roll Call

Then came the eagerly awaited Roll Call, the International Review, which Secretary Vogt happily conducted. He began with the foreign countries. For this summarized story we are indebted to the *Christian Endeavor World*: —

Miss Millar spoke for Australian Endeavorers: "We hope to meet all of you American Endeavorers in that land where there is no more sea." New South Wales sent a special greeting: "We are not divided, all one body we."

Our Bulgarian delegate spoke of the righteousness that exalteth a nation, and said, "We are standing for the best in this Christian Endeavor work."

For China, "the land of opportunity," Dr. Hallock spoke, first shaking hands with the audience Chinese fashion, by shaking his own hands and getting them to shake theirs.

Mr. Bonner spoke for the British delegates: "My comrades in work, and [turning to the chorus] my comrades in song, I have brought with me, as you have heard, an old friend, the very hammer which William Carey used a century ago. I pray that God may make this the symbol to hammer more closely those bonds of love which bind us to Jesus Christ and to one another."

For India, introduced by Mr. Hatch, the Misses Maya Das sang sweetly. The prayer of our Jamaican delegates was, "The joy of the Lord be your strength." Mr. Moses spoke well for Mexico. "The morning light is breaking" was Porto Rico's message.

Miss Ellen M. Stone, on behalf of her own Macedonia, said: "In that dark, sad land in which the captives languished and from which they were redeemed to freedom there are Christian Endeavorers. Pray that they may be able to stand, and, having done all, to stand."

Though grand receptions were given to all these foreign representatives, perhaps the heartiest greeting was given to our friends from Japan. Their message was: "In the midst of war we work for peace. The year's motto of our 126 societies is, 'Improve and Increase,' '*Kaizen, Kwakucho.*' Our counsel to you of the lands of the West is, 'Be strong in the Lord and in the strentgh of his might.' Harada, Kobe; Tamura, Tokyo; Pettee, Okayama; for the Japan Union of Christian Endeavor.'"

Many greetings were received, by cable, telegraph, and post. All of them were thoroughly enjoyed, evidencing as they did the world-wide spread of our delightful fellowship.

After he had done honor to other lands, we turned to our own. State yells had been excluded from this closing session, but the State songs and Scripture mottoes and other varied responses more than took their place in arousing enthusiasm. Repeatedly the audience would not allow a response to be completed before they burst into delighted applause. The delegations often stood on chairs that they might be seen and heard the better, and their waving banners, the beautiful new banners conspicuous among them, made a very lively sight.

Many of the delegations were unusually large, especially those from the Southern States, owing to our nearness to them.

Many of the States used Bible responses; here are some of them: Alaska, Illinois, and Delaware, "Forgetting the things that are behind," etc. Connecticut, "I am determined to know nothing among you save Jesus Christ." Florida, "Not to be ministered unto, but to minister." Ontario (whose delegation was almost entirely young men), "Seeing we are compassed about with so great a cloud of witnesses," etc. Indian Territory and Oklahoma, our Mizpah; Nebraska, "Not by might nor by power," etc. Oregon, "The Lord of hosts is with us," etc. Washington, "We shall labor to show ourselves approved unto God," etc. Iowa, "For God so loved the world," etc. The Floating societies, represented by Miss Jones and a sailor, "Though I take the wings of the morning, and dwell in the uttermost parts of the sea," etc.

"Colorado for Christ," "Christ for Louisiana," "Tennessee for Christ," "Texas for Christ," this was a frequent watchword.

The beautiful State songs are an ever-growing satisfaction in Christian Endeavor, and never have they sounded sweeter than at Baltimore. Georgia's "For Christ and for the Church we are singing" is to the tune of "Suwanee River." "For Christ and the Church, and our blest Endeavor band, in the old Kentucky home far away," is always a favorite. Maine's stirring song, to the tune of "Tramp, tramp, tramp," set all feet to literal tramping. Minnesota's song has an especially sweet refrain. New Hampshire has a fine State song, and so has Tennessee. The Michigan delegation aroused the perplexed interest of our hosts when they broke out with "Michigan, my Michigan," to the far-famed tune of "Maryland, my Maryland." "West Virginia hills" is one of the most charming and distinctive of these compositions. "Help save Ohio" and New York's "Sing on, sing on," to the tune of "Marching through Georgia," won delighted applause. But the chief enthusiasm was shown when Wisconsin sung "The Y. P. S. C. E. of Wisconsin" to the tune of "Dixie," and when our noble hosts, courteously withdrawn to the distant galleries that their guests might have the best places, sung with the chorus that loveliest of Christian Endeavor songs, "Maryland, my Maryland."

The *Sun* thus describes an incident of the roll-call: "No such scenes have ever been witnessed in Baltimore. The roll-call of the States and countries was a feature which it would be idle to describe. From forty-two States and from twelve foreign countries came the responses, each one gaining in earnestness and fervor over the other until Maryland, the last on the list, was reached. Then, as every Maryland man and woman in the building burst forth into their hymn, 'File into rank for Christ to-day,' singing it to the tune of 'Maryland, my Maryland,' the climax came, and with a roar that seemed to shake the foundations of the structure the enthusiasm broke loose."

But not always did the delegations use the State songs. Most tender effects were gained from some of our well-known hymns, and often only the initial measures would be sung, and the entire audience would join in with them. Thus, very appropriately, District of Columbia's stanza of "America," Illinois's "We will follow all the way," Indiana's "Jesus saves," "There's sunshine in my soul," from sunshiny Mississippi, New Jersey's "I'll go where you want me to go," "All hail, the power of Jesus' name" sung so pluckily by North Dakota's three delegates, Pennsylvania's great chorus of "Onward, Christian soldiers," and Iowa's "Nearer, my God, to Thee."

Still more variety was given to the fascinating service. Dr. Darby, for example, stood out from Indiana's company, and declared that Christian Endeavor in his State was now twenty-one years old, and inclined to show its independence, so that he intended to add to Dr. Clark's four propositions for the coming year a fifth, "One million new dollars as a tribute to our beloved leader, Dr. Clark." This sentiment was heartily cheered. Kansas made an allusion to the religious motive of its early settlement. Massachusetts took for its year's motto: "Unity and evangelism. He that winneth souls is wise." North Carolina thus interpreted the colors of its State banner. "Gold for sunshine, green for growth, and white for purity." Vermont proudly held out its six progress pennants, joined in an exhilarating line. Numbers of the States declared their intention to add to the stars on their increase banners. Missouri's motto: "More of Christ in me, to save the soul nearest me." New York's: "Great power for greater service."

It was Mr. Baer's part to speak the closing word.

"Alongside Dr. Clark's message to you and to me," he began, "will you please put this other sentence from President Roosevelt: 'The one thing supremely worth having is the opportunity coupled with the capacity to do a thing worthily and well, the doing of which in its final import touches all human kind.'" While this Convention will technically adjourn, it will only have begun as you carry its spirit out in your own lives. Let us take with us in our hearts these four purposes of Dr. Clark's. A chain is only as strong as its weakest link, and this chain of purpose belting the globe will be strong as you are strong, or will break with your lack of purpose. A million new Endeavorers for our societies! Can you say, 'We will'?"

"We will!" the Endeavorers answered.

"A million new church-members for our home churches!"

"*We will.*"

"A million new church-goers for our churches!"

"WE WILL!"

"A million new dollars for the cause of missions at home and abroad!"

"WE WILL!"

"And now as we leave these doors to go from the best Convention that Christian Endeavor has ever had, let us remember that the power of it will largely depend upon our work and our spirit. Let us wait before God in silence for His benediction, and let the last word be His."

Then, after a moment of most impressive quiet, we caught up our parting hymn, "God be with you till we meet again," and carried it out into the streets of Baltimore.

Christian Endeavor's Twenty-second International Convention was ended, — and was beginning.

BOAT LAKE, DRUID HILL PARK

A VIEW IN DRUID HILL PARK, BALTIMORE

CHAPTER XXII

Greetings From Many Lands

SENT TO THE BALTIMORE CHRISTIAN ENDEAVOR CONVENTION

We rejoice in the world-wide fellowship which Christian Endeavor affords, and in the interest it gives us in the progress of the kingdom of God everywhere.
E. H. BEANEY,
Hon. General Secretary of the South Australian Christian Endeavor Union.

We trust that the revival blessing which your States as well as ours are expectantly asking and believing for will come with mighty power.
HENRY BUSH,
Hon. General Secretary of the New South Wales Christian Endeavor Union.

"Sing unto the Lord a new song, and his praise from the end of the earth; ye that go down to the sea, and all that is therein, the isles and the inhabitants thereof." May your Convention be richly blessed.
LIZZIE BLACK,
Corresponding Secretary of the Dunedin and District Union, New Zealand.

Will you please convey the heartiest greetings of Irish Endeavorers to their sisters and brothers assembled in convention at Baltimore? We rejoice in the interdenominational and international fellowship made possible by the Society, and pray that Christian Endeavor may bind all the nations of the earth with the golden chain of prayer and love about the feet of God.
J. NEWMAN HALL,
Hon. Secretary of the Irish Christian Endeavor Union.

May the Lord richly bless your Twenty-second International Convention at Baltimore for the good of all nations. We, too, of the Russian Baltic Christian Endeavor Society, intend with God's help to hold our first convention of the Russian Baltic Christian Endeavor Society in Rujen, Livonia, on June 19.
REV. ROBERT BAHTZ,
Field Secretary of the Russian Baltic Christian Endeavor Union.

The Christian Endeavorers of China, organized in three hundred and fifty societies, connected with twenty-four mission boards, in fifteen provinces, send from their sixth national convention at Ningpo to the Endeavorers gathered at the International Convention in Baltimore a most hearty greeting, a note of praise for what God has done for us through Christian Endeavor, and a confident summons to join with us in bringing China to Christ.
REV. GEORGE W. HINMAN,
General Secretary of the United Society of Christian Endeavor for China.

The wishes of the German Christian Endeavor Union for some of the great Conventions of this year:

Baltimore / Birmingham / Berlin { the same Master / the same Holy Ghost / the same principles / the same pledge / the same goals / the same victory } Upward! / Inward! / Onward!

REV. FRIEDRICH BLECHER,
Secretary of the German Christian Endeavor Union.

The Orient greets the Occident once more. The new Christian Endeavor Union of old India sends renewed messages of gratitude to the mother of us all, and of loyalty to the principles for which Christian Endeavor stands.

REV. WILLIAM I. CHAMBERLAIN, D.D., and REV. L. B. CHAMBERLAIN,
President and Honorary General Secretary of the United Society of Christian Endeavor in India, Burma, and Ceylon.

In this sunny land we feel there is much lying in shadow still to be possessed, and the buoyant hopefulness which has characterized our gatherings at our late Convention is the guaranty that the frontier line of Christian Endeavor will be extended in the coming year. We pray that this joyful experience of extension may be shared by all lands. With our hearty greetings and prayers that, strong in the strength which cometh down from above, you may find the coming year one of glorious achievement.

MILDRED CLEGHORN,
Secretary of the Christian Endeavor Union of South Africa.

The Convention of the Samoa Christian Endeavor Union [embracing the Tokelau and Ellice Islands] sends greetings to the International Convention of the United Society of Christian Endeavor at Baltimore, congratulates the United Society on the manifest tokens of God's blessing which all our societies throughout the world continue to receive, and prays that great grace may rest upon the officers and trustees, and that the Convention may fulfil all their highest hopes, and that the issue of all our gatherings may be the world-wide evangelization of our race for whom Christ died.

JAMES E. NEWELL, *President.*
SAAGA, *Secretary.*

Greetings in Jesus' name. He does well who gives his money to aid a good work, but he does better who gives himself to the work. The Master deserves our best effort.

LOLA V. MURPHY,
Superintendent of Prison Work for Iowa.

We, the members of the Prison Christian Endeavor Society of the Iowa State Penitentiary at Anamosa, extend to you our heartfelt sympathy in, and appreciation of, your work, and assure you that our prayer is for your success in your consultations and deliberations for the cause of world-wide Christian Endeavor. In your supplications to the throne of grace remember us, who may seem to be such unworthy mites in the great Endeavor movement.

WILLIAM TOOL, *President,*
OTIS GREEN, *Secretary,*
J. W. HOOT, *Secretary,*
Committee of the Iowa State Penitentiary Society.

From Spain, this: "If God be for us, who can be against us?" "It is our Father's pleasure to give us the kingdom."

REV. WILLIAM H. GULICK, D.D.

The Convention was glad to receive the following: "Greetings from Prohibition National Committee. Christian Endeavor is America's hope in her irrepressible conflict with the liquor traffic. Hit hard in God's name."

CHARLES R. JONES, *Chairman.*

"California Union sends its greetings. Isa. 41:6 ('They helped every one his neighbor, and every one said to his neighbor, Be of good courage')."

The following cablegram was received from the European Convention at Berlin: "Europe's united Endeavorers' hopeful greetings to America." The following reply was sent: "America and Europe united by the cable of Christian Endeavor."

This cablegram came from the Antipodes: "New South Wales to beautiful Baltimore:

"'We are not divided,
All one body we,
One in hope and doctrine,
One in charity.'

All returns not yet in, but a goodly number of societies report ten-per-cent gain."

"Idaho Convention sends greetings, appealing for the next Convention to come West, preferring Seattle.

J. M. ELLIS."

"Kindly extend to all Endeavorers at the Convention hearty greetings from the Intermediates of our Chicago Christian Endeavor Union."

C. C. BROWN, *Superintendent.*

CHAPTER XXIII

The Evangelistic Work

THERE was a systematic evangelistic work carried on by this Convention, exceeding anything hitherto attempted. Two skilled leaders like Mr. Biederwolf and Mr. Stelzle gave dignity and importance to the movement, and they not only spoke in conferences and conducted the great mass meeting for men, but held daily services at noon and in the evening. At noon services were held at the Baltimore Copper Works and the Ohio Railroad Shops, where the men listened most respectfully and attentively each day, and there were many expressions of conviction and interest.

On Saturday afternoon a power houseboat, *Reliance*, was transformed into a Gospel Boat by the Evangelistic Committee, and took out about fifty Endeavor workers, speakers and singers, for a cruise in the harbor.

Rev. Thomas M. Readenkoff, of the Evangelistic Meetings' committee, had charge. Prominent among the speakers was Miss Antoinette P. Jones, of Falmouth, Mass., corresponding secretary of the Floating Christian Endeavor Societies, who has had much experience among seamen in her Northern home.

Stops were made, short talks given, and hymns sung at the foot of Hughes Street, at the Johnston Line steamer Templemore, Pier 34, Locust Point, and at the Northern Central ore pier, Lower Canton, where the British steamer Cunaxa is berthed.

A stop followed off the French steamer Jurien de la Graviere, when the Endeavorers sang several of their hymns before leaving for Fort Howard, where a meeting was held about 6.30 P. M. Colonel Thorpe, the commandant, gave permission to address the members of the Coast Artillery at the post.

Evening meetings were arranged for in the market places of the city. Among the speakers were Miss Millar, of Australia, Messrs. Biederwolf and Stelzle, Rev. C. L. Evarts, of Boston, Rev. W. T. Patchell, of California, and others. The bad weather interfered with the plans for outdoor meetings, though a number were held. Thousands in Baltimore heard the gospel and will remember Christian Endeavor. It was noted that everywhere there was the utmost respect and courtesy. This runs through all classes.

THE PRISON WORKERS

The rally in the interests of Prison Christian Endeavor was held on Sunday afternoon in the Harlem Avenue Christian Church, and made a strong showing for this advancing department of work, a work in many ways most remarkable. It seems odd at first thought to be told that one of the largest Endeavor societies in the world is in a penitentiary.

Chaplain A. G. Gates, of the Kansas Industrial Reformatory; Miss Lucy Starling, prison superintendent of the Kentucky Christian Endeavor Union; Warden Charles A. Hook, of the Baltimore city jail; and Rev. J. J. Burkhart, superintendent of the Maryland Prisoners' Aid Society, emphasized from their own observation the power of Christ's love and the love of Christians in making of prisoners new men in Christ Jesus.

The closing address by the presiding officer, Rev. Edward A. Fredenhagen, of Topeka, Kan., the devoted general superintendent of the Societies for the Friendless, set forth and illustrated the "Fundamentals of Prison Endeavor" as expressed by the four watchwords, "Adaptation," "Evangelization," "Nurture," "Restoration." Like the other speakers he made an effective appeal for greater efforts in this neglected but promising field.

Captain Gates, an enthusiast in this work, said: —

> Some call a prisoner an abandoned man, in incurable, a pervert, a criminal, and some call him a convict. The prisoner, through the aid of the workers from the Christian Endeavor Prison Societies, is taught the word of Christ, is taught His beloved teachings, and there he becomes imbued with the spirit of the Saviour. There are prisoners in the penitentiaries and other reformatories throughout this country who will have a better chance before God when they face Him on His great white throne than hundreds of men outside the institutions who profess to be real Christians.
>
> Prisoners in all institutions are taught the gospel, taught to love Jesus, and when they are consecrated to Christ within the prison walls they release all of their wrongdoings from their heart and wholly accept Christ as their Saviour. When a prisoner is released from his confinement he should not be looked upon as a convict, pervert or criminal, but you Christian Endeavorers, who say you have the love of Jesus in your hearts, should extend a sociable hand to him, take him and encourage him, acknowledge him as a brother of yours and one who is working for the same cause you are — the salvation of other souls.

Miss Starling said: "I have yet to find the prisoner who could not be reached by love." She exhibited some banners which the prisoners of the Kentucky institutions who are members of the Christian Endeavor made during their stay behind the bars. She urged Christian Endeavorers to take a firmer hold on prison work, encourage the man who once wore the stripes and help him on his heavenly way after he leaves the institution. She read some expressions from prisoners who have accepted Christ. Some of the expressions are: —

> God has been so good to me. I never had any rest until he gave it to me. I want you to pray for me, that I may not look back any more.
>
> We have a great many who were raised among such wicked environments that their lives are extremely hard to change. It is only by coming in touch with some pure, sweet lives and hearing the love of Jesus that these can be reached.
>
> There is a great work to be done here. One need not go farther to do mission work nor to find souls to reclaim.
>
> Without Jesus this would be a miserable place indeed. But in serving God here we find many sweet hours and rays of sunshine.

Miss Starling, in commenting on the testimonials, said: —

Many times have I seen tears course down some cheek at the reading of a Christian letter from some Christian Endeavor friend. Many times have I seen countenances of sorrow turned to joy by being given a book or a flower or even a kind recognition. These are some of the things an outside Christian Endeavor friend can do to make a sad heart happy. You have no idea how many friendless men are here. There is no class of men so susceptible to the gentle touch and kind words as the prisoner. Our society (Frankfort, white) is in better spiritual condition to-day than it has ever been.

A Round of Prisons

In a steady downpour of rain, but singing "There is sunshine in my soul" and "There shall be showers of blessing," four hundred Endeavorers under the guidance of Rev. J. J. Burkhart, superintendent of the Maryland Prisoners' Aid Society, set out for a visit to penal institutions in the city.

Warden John F. Weyler, of the Maryland Penitentiary, personally met and welcomed the visitors and conducted them through the institution, explaining at length its working.

Warden Charles A. Hook, with his deputy and clerk, met the visitors at the city jail, and escorted them, showing the methods of administration.

At both institutions the wardens made addresses, and after the inspection the delegation held a song service in the chapel of the jail. A vote of thanks was passed for the kind and hearty welcome, and approval was expressed of the spirit of helpfulness and reformation that was found at both places.

CHAPTER XXIV

Convention Features

THE CHRISTIAN ENDEAVOR MUSEUM

Always an attraction at the Conventions, Mr. Holley's Christian Endeavor Museum this year had an exceptionally favorable place for display, so that visitors could examine its treasures to the best advantage. This collection of badges, programs, flags, and literature of Christian Endeavor from all lands has often been described. But it is continually growing, so that there is always something new to be seen. Various additions were made at Baltimore. Some of the interesting recent gains were a fine Irish flag woven especially for Mr. Holley at the request of a correspondent in Ireland, a small Icelandic flag with its white falcon painted on it by hand, and a metal K such as is worn for a badge by many Endeavorers among the French convicts on the Loyalty Islands.

The Missionary Museum

An exhibit of great value and interest for all missionary committees and other students of missions was the Missionary Museum to be found in the Lyric in charge of Mr. Harry S. Myers, the secretary of missionary work among the Free Baptist young people.

Here had been systematically arranged missionary text-books, pamphlets, leaflets, maps, charts, concert exercises, periodicals, literature for use with Juniors and in Sunday schools, catalogues of pictures and stereopticon slides, prayer cycles and calendars, and leaflets on giving.

The home and foreign and woman's boards of the different denominations were represented in the collection. Besides these there was literature of the Student Volunteer Movement and the Young People's Missionary Movement.

No one in search of new materials or methods for mission-study could fail of finding help there.

The Baltimore Committee

Brainy business men and ministers composed a committee that left nothing undone which made for the smooth running and sure success of the Convention, so far as perfect arrangement and management could do it. Indebtedness to this splendid committee, which had worked hard for twenty months, was happily recognized at the banquet given in their honor at the Hotel Belvedere by the Board of Trustees of the United Society. With invited guests, a company of nearly seventy sat down to the feast of good things, for an hour of social relaxation and enjoyment.

1907 Convention

Cordial invitations were received for the 1907 Convention from Kansas City, Mo., Minneapolis, Seattle, and Los Angeles. It was voted to refer the matter to the Executive Committee, with instructions to secure information as to the advisability of holding the Convention in cooler weather, and any other matters of interest, and report at a later meeting of the Board of Trustees.

What do you say about a spring, fall, or winter Convention? Write your views to the United Society of Christian Endeavor, Boston, Mass.

The Convention Badge

The Convention badge, designed by Mr. Spencer E. Sisco, chairman of the committee on halls, was by far the most elaborate and beautiful we have had. A gilt metal cross with a kind of trefoil at the end of each arm bore on its face "Baltimore, 1905," and in white in the center the Christian Endeavor monogram. To the cross was attached a ribbon of Maryland's colors, black and yellow. This formed the background for a shield hanging from the cross. This shield bore, in enamel of black and yellow, red and white, a part of the coat of arms of Lord Baltimore; and on it was a raised representation of the Battle Monument from the city seal, the monument commemorating the victory in the War of 1812 that saved Baltimore from British invasion.

Aside from the beauty of the badge and its relations to the history of State and city, a symbolism appropriate to Christian Endeavor was found in the heraldic symbols, while the whole was considered as illustrating the text, "Righteousness exalteth a nation."

The division of the shield by the perpendicular bands is emblematic of a fort, a reminder that "a mighty fortress is our God." The cross with its budding arms, said to represent the budding virtues of a youthful champion, was fitly worn by an army of Christian young people. The shield, divided into four parts, pictures a shield broken in battle, significant of the bearer's bravery, and recalls the good fight that is to be fought.

Note. In response to many inquiries from those who were unable to be present at the Convention, the United Society has made arrangements by which they can furnish the badge to Endeavorers at the low cost of ten cents each. Address, The United Society of Christian Endeavor, Tremont Temple, Boston.

CHAPTER XXV

The Convention Aftermath

Here are some of the interesting bits picked up by the Convention wayside. They are sidelights on such a vast gathering, and the city in which it was held, and properly belong with the report, although not strictly a part of it.

A Moody Convert Detective

Detective Tod Hall, the evangelist, who dropped into a Moody meeting many years ago in the old Maryland Institute and went away converted, was detailed at the Armory all week, and had the time of his life.

"This is the most remarkable religious gathering ever held in this city," he said enthusiastically yesterday afternoon, waving his arms and smiling.

Other members of the detective force have been at the Armory, too, but with "Detective Tod," as he is called, it has been a plain case of recreation and enjoyment.

"I have enjoyed every minute of it," he said, "and I don't care how long it lasts. This is a good crowd to be in. They are good citizens. If all the people were like them the police and detectives would have to look for new jobs."

Fragrant and Gracious, Baltimorean

At the meeting at the Associate Congregationalist Church Friday afternoon a white rose was presented to every one that attended. Some one thousand roses were distributed, and on the program Dr. Huckel, the pastor, had inscribed an appropriate verse, which ran as follows:

> A thousand roses, fragrant, white, and fair,
> May all your paths be strewn with roses fair;
> May all your lives breathe rose bloom on the air,
> In happy songs, kind deeds, and loving prayer.

Appreciative Guests

St. Paul's English Lutheran Church was the scene of a graceful presentation. The Massachusetts delegation, which has been making its headquarters at St. Paul's, presented the young people of the church and Rev. P. A. Heilman, the pastor, a picture of "The Sailing of the Mayflower." Mr. George E. Copeland, President of the Massachusetts Union, in a few remarks voiced the deep appreciation of the Massachusetts Endeavorers for the many courtesies which the kind thoughtfulness of the young people and the pastor had provided for their comfort and cheer.

The Trustees to Dr. Clark

The following resolution on the illness of Dr. Clark was offered by Dr. James L. Hill, who was authorized to communicate the same to Dr. Clark:

The United Society of Christian Endeavor, assembled amid splendid, complete, and unsurpassed preparation for this, the Twenty-second International Convention, finishing twenty-four years of radiant history of Christian Endeavor service, learns with deep regret that our eminent and beloved natural leader, Dr. Francis E. Clark, is not present through temporary illness, exemplifying the deep meaning of the text, "The good of thine house hath eaten me up."

We unite in our prayers and our love in sending him our good wishes, and we join in the petition that his illness may be brief, and that he may prosper and be in health, even as his soul prospereth.

Chairman Atwood "Takes the Cake"

After Chairman Atwood had delivered his adress of welcome and returned to his seat he was handed a neatly wrapped package. It was wrapped in tissue paper and held fast by red and white ribbons, the Convention colors. The package was an angel cake, made from flour taken from the souvenir bags of the cereal brought to the Convention by the delegates from Minneapolis. The young ladies of the city on committees of the Convention presented the chairman with the cake, and a card bearing the following was tied to the ribbons: "For Mr. Atwood: Compliments of Baltimore girls."

The Handy Lunch Room

This was a boon to thousands. Between five and six thousand meals daily were served in the lunchroom conducted by the Woman's Exchange at the Armory. Sandwiches, tea, coffee, milk, pie, cake and ice-cream disappeared as if by magic, and the hot meals served in the middle of the day had a wide popularity.

The Endeavorers apparently left their sweet teeth at home, for the candy booth did not carry off many of their shekels. But for the toothsome pie and the substantial sandwich they have shown an abiding liking. Ice-cream has been a close second to pie in popularity, and grape-juice and ginger ale have been much in demand as thirst quenchers.

Sunrise on Lookout Mountain

The Tennessee delegates had a charming experience en route to Baltimore, as told in this dispatch:

"Massed on the eastern edge of the summit of historic old Lookout Mountain several hundred Christian workers witnessed the rising of the sun and bowed their heads in silence as President J. H. Race, of Grant University, invoked the divine blessing and spoke of a supplication for universal peace. Dr. Ira Landrith, of Nashville, delivered a patriotic and religious address on the 'Patriotism of Peace.'

"The meeting was held under the auspices of the Young People's Religious Societies of Lookout Mountain and Chattanooga for the delegates to the Christian Endeavor Convention in Baltimore. A large number of delegates, together with their Chattanooga hosts, spent the night on the mountain."

Able and Accommodating

Chairman Henry Gilligan of the press committee was one of the busiest and most obliging committeemen in the lists. Not infrequently he rivaled the multiple accomplishments of Poet Louis Michel, writing an order with one hand, working the typewriter with the other, dictating a letter and kicking something out of his way, with his feet — all at one time and smilingly, as though it didn't bother him. A true Endeavor gentleman.

Courtesy and Helpfulness

The Baltimore conductor has received a good share of the comment on the city and its institutions by the visiting delegates. Most of them are complimentary.

"Our conductor certainly was accommodating," said one, who had been in a party seeing the burnt district. "He even showed us the place the fire started."

"Baltimore is not a difficult town to get about in, when you know enough to inquire of the natives," said a member of the New York delegation. "The policemen are very obliging, too, but the way the citizen will go out of the way to do a stranger a favor is surprising. One of our delegates, an old man, forgot where he had left a package down town the other day and a man on the street helped him to search for half an hour until the store was located."

The Generous Jap

Mr. Ogawa, the Japanese, who is in this country studying at Oberlin College, Ohio, and who is a delegate to the Convention, was one of the few in the audience to applaud when Secretary Vogt referred to Russia and her advancement in the Christian Endeavor field. Russia is greatly on the increase in Christian Endeavor work, and Mr. Ogawa clapped his hands in approval of the results in the country now in bitter conflict with his native land.

Fully Equipped Hospital

The hospital was one of the best places about the Armory. Here Dr. William Dulany Thomas, 633 North Carrollton Avenue, assisted by a corps of physicians and two trained nurses — Miss Anna Short, head nurse, and Miss Carneal — looked after delegates suffering from heat, fatigue of travel, or any other ill. The hospital was fitted up, even to appliances for surgical operations. About fifty persons were treated, no cases serious.

To Guard Against Fire

Firemen were stationed in the hall with several hand extinguishers. Four lines of hose, reaching to all parts of the Armory, were attached and ready for instant use.

"There won't be any fire," said Chief Horton: "but we are prepared, anyway."

INDEX

	PAGE
American Indians	56
Annual Address	113
Baltimore's Welcome	
By the Mayor	19
By Rev. Oliver Huckel, for the Pastors	19
By W. O. Atwood, Chairman of the Committee of 1905	20
Banners, State and Union	104
Bible Recitations	39
Brotherhood of Christian Endeavor	55
Bulgaria	59
Canada	57
Camp-fire, Christian Endeavor	82
China	56
Christian Citizenship	111
Christian Culture	75
Christian Endeavor	
Annual Statistical Record	21, 22
Increase and Betterment	21, 22
Fellowship	25
Floating Endeavor	40
Federation of Unions	40
Quarter-Century Review	42
Financial Management	82
President's Review for the Year	115
Motto given for the coming Year	119
Principles Restated	123
Christian Endeavor in Picture, Song and Story	59
Christian Endeavor Flag Song	53
Christian Schools, need of	77
Church-going	117
Committee of 1905	120, 133
Conscience, Education of	75
Consecration Meetings	86
Convention, 1907	134
Convention, Baltimore	
The Armory	8
New System of Registration	8
Numbers Present	10
Lyric Hall	10
The Audiences	8
Decorations and Electrical Effects	9, 26
Varied Features of	133, 137
Badge, description of	134
Convention Chorus	13, 26

	PAGE
Denominational Rallies	
Joint Presbyterian	63
Baptist	63
Congregational	64
Lutheran	64
Reformed Church in America	65
African Methodist Episcopal and African Methodist Episcopal Zion	65
Methodist Protestant	65
Disciples	66
United Evangelical	66
United Brethren	66
Reformed Church in the United States	67
Episcopalian	67
Joint Methodist	67
United and Reformed Presbyterians	68
Brethren	68
Reformed Episcopalian	69
Friends	69
Church of God	69
Free Baptists	70
Moravians	70
Endeavor Flag Song	53
Endeavor Hymnal	78
England	57
Epworth League	
Greeting sent to	52
Response from	84
Evangelism	7, 71, 130
Session devoted to	71
Evangelization	115
Evangelistic Services	130
Evangelistic Appeal to Men	91
Flag Exercise	52
Flag Song	84
Gettysburg, Visit to	80
Address at	81
Greetings from Many Lands	127
Hospitality	11
Hospital	137
Hymn, "Christian Endeavor"	6
Increase Movement	22, 23, 104
India	57
Jamaica	56
Japan	56, 57, 59

139

INDEX

	PAGE
Junior Endeavor	
For the Boys and Girls	42
Junior Rally	47
Junior Chorus	54
Boys' and Girls' Meeting	95
Life Preserver, The, Illustrated talk	49
Maryland	
Welcome by Governor	18
Endeavor Hymn	19, 53
Men's Meeting	89
Messages	
From Dr. Clark	15, 51, 107, 114
From Mrs. Clark	51, 86, 93
To Dr. Clark	27, 71
To Mrs. Clark	94
From President Roosevelt	17
To President Roosevelt	17
Missions, Study of	35, 36
Music	
Character of at Convention	8
Praise of the Nations	26
Story of Endeavor in Song	48
Music in the Society	78
Museums, Christian Endeavor and Missionary	133
Pastor as an Evangelist	73
Pennant Presentation	103
Personal Purity Reform	98
Political Reform	109
Porto Rico	56
Praise of the Nations	26
Press of Baltimore	
Excellent Reports and Sympathetic Spirit of	12
Prison Work	131
Public Opinion, Responsibility for	111
Quarter-Century Testimonial	61, 62, 83, 84
Quiet Hour	31
Recognition Meeting	101
Reforms	98–100, 108–112
Resolutions and Statement of Principles	121
Roll Call of States	113, 124
Roll of Honor	102
Sabbath Reform	99
School of Methods	
Christian Endeavor Methods	33
Pastors' Conferences	34
Home Mission Study Class	35
Foreign Mission Study Class	36
Personal Work	37
Christian Culture	37
Junior Conferences	38
Bible Recitals	39
State and Local Union Conferences	40
State Responses at Roll Call	124, 125
Story of Endeavor in Song	48
State Banners	104
State Rallies	61
Sunday Services	86
Sunshine Talk	95
Washington, Celebration at	79
Woman's Meeting	93
Workingmen and the Church	90, 108
World's Convention, Geneva	57

PERSONNEL

Abratani, Jiro	56, 88
Akrabova, Evanka S.	59, 94
Albert, Mary E.	66
Arnett, B. W.	55, 65
Atchison, T. C.	68
Atwood, W. O.	18, 20, 65
Baer, John Willis	113, 115, 119, 126
Baker, Smith	20
Bagby, E. B.	66
Bartholomew, A. R.	67
Bauman, L. S.	68
Beckley, J. T.	63
Beelman, Grace	49
Biederwolf, W. E.	34, 89, 90, 91, 92, 130
Bonner, Carey	26, 29, 95, 121
Bonaparte, C. J.	109
Brokaw, R. W.	42
Burkhart, J. J.	131
Carpenter, G. C.	68
Clark, F. E.	7, 15, 27, 51, 113, 114
Clark, Mrs. F. E.	38, 51, 93
Clements, John R.	34, 87
Clews, C.	67
Copp, Z. H.	68
Davidson, Nellie A.	48
Darby, W. J.	63, 71
Delk, E. H.	64
Dunlap, J. F.	66
Duxbury, John	39
Eckert, C. H.	66
Eggleston, G. H.	65
Esler, Alexander	57
Evarts, C. L.	37, 131
Fallows, Samuel	69, 80
Foster, Percy S.	8, 58, 114
Freer, Harris	65
Fredenhagen, E. A.	131
Gaines, A. L.	65
Gates, A. G.	131
Gifford, O. P.	63, 72
Girardin, J. B.	66
Gladden, Washington	64, 73
Goucher, John F.	68
Graff, George B.	57
Grose, Howard B.	15, 27, 63
Grove, C. A.	69
Hadlock, E. H.	33

INDEX

	PAGE
Hallenbeck, W. H.	40, 63
Hallock, H. G. C.	56, 59
Harker, Amanda	19
Harris, R. A.	69, 93
Haslup, R. L.	59
Hatch, F. S.	57, 64, 66
Haus, Kate	38, 45
Hay, John	16
Heilman, P. A.	64
Heisse, J. F.	60
Hewett, E. J.	56, 64
Hicks, H. W.	36
Hill, J. L.	27, 48, 66, 80, 101, 121
Hill, Mrs. J. L.	38, 93
Hodgdon, Mrs. H. H.	38
Hootman, A. S.	64
Howe, J. L.	63, 75
Hubbell, C. H.	46, 66
Huckel, O.	19
Hume, R. A.	31, 57, 64
Humphries, E.	65
Hulm, George	69
Jacobs, F. H.	8, 42, 56, 75, 101, 106
Jones, Antoinette P.	40
Kenngott, George H.	38
Key, Alicia	107
King, H. C.	31
Knipp, J. E.	88
Koch, Margaret	37, 95
Landrith, Ira	55, 56, 87
Lathrop, H. N.	57, 64
Leland, J. S.	66
Lewis, T. H.	66
McAllister, J. A.	56
McElveen, W. T.	45, 64
McMillan, W. H.	46, 68, 98
McNaugher, S.	68, 100
Macfarland, B. F.	111
Maten, D. S.	65
Matthews, M. A.	73
May, Dr.	69
Maya Das, Dora Mohinie	57, 94
Maya Das, Ethel Merian	57, 94
Michener, C. C.	37
Millar, E. Stafford	31, 94
Miller, R. G.	67
Mills, J. S.	65
Mohn, Otto L. F.	65
Myers, Harry S.	70
Ogawa, C.	59, 84
Ohrum, S. C.	63

	PAGE
Olney, Elizabeth W.	38
Palmer, C. J.	67
Patchell, W. T.	130
Phillputt, Alan B.	58
Poling, C. C.	66
Porter, H. W.	48
Post, Emma	48
Power, F. D.	16, 71, 106
Price, H. M.	69
Randall, J. E.	83
Reed, Elizabeth	66
Reichard, L. S.	66
Roosevelt, Theodore	16, 17
Russell, Elbert	69
Schumacher, W. A.	67
Scott, O. J. W.	65
Shaw, William	16, 17, 27, 33, 40, 42, 82, 120
Shelton, Don O.	35, 83, 88
Shupe, H. F.	66
Smith, E. Tennyson	109
Stanford, W. M.	66
Starling, Lucy	131
Stelzle, Charles	63, 90, 108, 130
Stewart, George B.	16, 34, 42, 58, 63
Stone, Ellen M.	52, 94
Stone, John Timothy	63
Stout, L. E.	69
Straughn, J. H.	65
Suter, Mrs. Antoinette	39
Swift, Albert	44, 57
Timanus, Mayor	19
Thompson, E. W.	65
Tomkins, Floyd W.	15, 44, 67
Tyndall, C. H.	49
Vogler, W. H.	70
Vogt, Von Ogden	21, 34, 40, 99, 104
Waggoner, J. M.	69
Walters, Alexander	55, 65
Warfield, Governor	17
Wells, Amos R.	64, 84
Wevill, Duane	69
Wilbur, H. W.	98
Williams, J. E.	69
Williams, Nellie	39
Williams, P. H.	65
Wilson, A. W.	68
Wood-Allen, Mary	98
Wylie, R. C.	68, 99
Yoder, C. F.	68

www.ingramcontent.com/pod-product-compliance
Lightning Source LLC
Chambersburg PA
CBHW031354040426
42444CB00005B/281